A

Marese Hickey has do Moth in New Zealand, with wild dolphins in t ... is an energy master healer, holistic therapist and former nurse. She has worked as a clinical hypnotherapist for seventeen years. Marese has known love and loss, sorrow and joy. Now that she loves herself, she would like to help others do the same. She is also an animal healer and servant to four cats. The most famous of these is Harry Three Paws, who even wrote his own blog for a while despite the absence of opposable furry thumbs. You can visit her blog and website on www.maresehickey.com and receive the gift of a meditation download called "Letting Go and Feeling Good" when you sign up for emails about new releases.

Copyright notice

ISBN-13 9781523264650
ISBN-10 1523264659

Copyright © Marese Hickey 2016

All rights reserved. No part of this publication may be reproduced, translated, adapted, stored in a retrieval system or transmitted, in any form or by any means, including electronic, mechanical, photocopying, or recording without the prior written permission of the author, nor be otherwise circulated in any form of binding or cover other than that in which it is published and without a similar condition being imposed on the purchaser.

Author's Note and Disclaimer
The ideas and suggestions in this book are not intended as a substitute for consulting with a counsellor, psychologist or mental health professional. If you have experienced severe trauma, it is advisable to get appropriate professional help.

Cover design by Kat Ennis. Artist.
https://www.facebook.com/Kat-Ennis-Artist
Email: kat.ennis@yahoo.com

www.maresehickey.com

Dedication
To my beloved peaceful people
Dad, Gran, Gannet and Izzy

How to Love Yourself in Less Than 50 Years

A gentle, compassionate and effective starter kit

Marese Hickey

HTP Books

Contents

Chapter 1 The Magic Elixir 1

How Long Does It Take to Love Yourself? 1
What Qualifies Me to Write About This? 3
When is a Good Time to Start? 3
How Will Loving Myself Improve My Life? 4
So Loving Myself Will Solve All My Problems? 4
How Do We Become Unloving To Ourselves? 5
The Culture of Fear 5
The Early Rocky Road - What We Need and What We Get 6
Roles and Masks 7
Dissociation 7
The Energy Battery 8
Assessment: Where Am I Now? 9
Exercise: Sit and Breathe 10

Chapter 2 Making a Start 13

Set Your Intention 13
The First Step 15
Excavation 16
Growing Self Awareness through Enquiry 17
Appreciation 17
Appreciation Inventory 18
Exercise: Self-Appreciation 19

Chapter 3 Making Space to Be Yourself 21

Letting Go and Getting Out of The Way 21
Letting Go of Perfectionism 23
Letting Go of Mistakes and Hurts 23
Feng Shui: Combining Physical Action with Mental Intention 24
Puja: Ritual for Letting Go 25

Chapter 4 Nourishment 27

Physical Nourishment 27
Emotional Nourishment 30
Spiritual Nourishment 33

Mental Nourishment 35
Visualisation: Discovering the Treasure Within 40

Chapter 5 Recovering Your Power 41

Waiting for the Prince on a White Horse 41
Blame versus Responsibility 42
Life Review 43
Forgiveness 44
Exercise: Forgiveness 45

Chapter 6 Releasing Fear 47

Overcoming Negativity 48
Imagination and Self-Talk 52
The Stop Light Technique 53
Recognising Truth 53
Visualisation: The Safe Place 55

Chapter 7 Light hearted and Light footed 57

The Power of Humour and Play 57
Healing Through Dance and Movement 58
Your Challenge 62

Chapter 8 Becoming Still To Learn: Mindfulness 63

The Gifts of Mindfulness 65
Emotions and Mindfulness 71
About the Body Scan 72
Exercise: The Body Scan 74

Chapter 9 Getting Through Grief and Loss 77

Gentler Questions 80
Visualisation: Lovingkindness Meditation 83

Chapter 10 Resurrecting Dreams and Living Your Life Purposefully 85

Soul Purpose 85
Being and Doing 87
Investigating What We Want 89
Service 90
Exercise: Discovering What Is Important 91

Chapter 11 Becoming Authentic 93
- *Who Am I?* 93
- *Speaking Out From the Heart* 94
- *The Blues* 95
- *Integrity* 97
- *Acknowledging the Shadow Self* 98
- *Freedom* 100
- *Permission* 100
- *Practice and the Ego* 101
- *Your Challenge* 103

Chapter 12 Gathering Resources for the Journey 105
- *Abundance and Prosperity* 105
- *Letting Go of Scarcity* 106
- *The Sequence of Manifestation* 108
- *Gratitude* 111
- *The Shape of Help* 113
- *What will you allow?* 114
- *Visualisation: Attracting and Allowing Abundance* 115

Chapter 13 Near Death Experiences and Near Life Opportunities 117
- *Learning from Death* 117
- *Aligning with our God-Self* 118
- *A New Way of Being in the World* 119
- *Visualisation: Integrating the Positive Changes* 120

References 122

Suggested Reading and Resources 123

Acknowledgements 124

Chapter 1

The Magic Elixir

*Plant your own garden and decorate your own soul,
instead of waiting for someone to bring you flowers.*
Veronica A. Shoffstall

Imagine you could buy a potion that promised to increase your vital energy, knock years off your face by causing you to smile and laugh more and that would generally transform your life for the better. There would be a stampede to buy it! Well, here's the secret: loving yourself is the magic elixir. And we can all have it!

If you have chosen to read this book, it is because the title and subject resonate with you at some level. That part of you is your soul, which longs for expression through experience. Truth and authenticity are the song of your soul. The Universe longs to express itself through you, joyfully and abundantly, dancing you into a state of happiness.

The physics of cosmology tells us that the Universe was born infinite. Everywhere that is here now was there at the moment of the Big Bang 13.75 billion years ago. Space-time has been expanding and stretching ever since. Every carbon atom in every living thing on the planet was produced in the heart of a dying star. We are literally made of stardust. Your soul also came from the Universe and is made of the same stuff, and has the same tendency towards infinite expansion and growth.

How Long Does It Take to Love Yourself?

It is possible to change your life in an instant, a day or a week, but sustaining that change is the real challenge. It is like the difference between starting a diet and staying on it until you achieve your goal. By the time you have achieved that goal, the plan is that you will have a new set of beliefs and behaviours that allow you to sustain the positive changes. I am hoping that you will be able to love yourself in less than fifty years. If not, it takes as long as it takes.

The Irish healer, Michael Doherty, wrote about how bio energy healing was effective in alleviating conditions for many people – however, afterwards, sometimes the client's condition worsened again.[1] The reason for this is that a healer can only do so much, and then it is up to the client to make the positive changes to support that work. Without that "change work," the effect of the healing dissipates.

Why might we be unwilling or unable to make the necessary positive changes? Our routines are what make us feel safe, so change can be uncomfortable and there is a universal resistance to it. Sometimes it is also because we have "secondary gain" from illness or staying stuck. If we are on sick leave from a job that we hate, for example, we may subconsciously sabotage the effort to get well. We may be in unhealthy relationships that we know are not good for us, but we are afraid of change, because "The devil you know is better than the one you don't." Relationships like these depend on all parties staying the same. The unwritten rule is that nobody changes. If one person changes, it throws a spanner in the works.

Loving yourself is the first step on the road to living more consciously. This book is about the journey to your authentic, true self. When you become able to love yourself, you become your *real*, *best*, and *highest* self. When this happens, you will know it. You will know because you will feel much more calm and peaceful inside, for more of the time. You will feel comfortable in your own skin perhaps for the first time ever. You will feel more grounded, more contented, energetic and joyful. This is your natural state, and your soul has been singing you home to it, all of your life.

What Qualifies Me to Write About This?

I was not able to love myself for a long, long time. Now that I do, I feel great and with the zeal of a convert, I want everyone to feel as good as I do! I'm also more than fifty years old. I am a clinical hypnotherapist with seventeen years' experience in the field of managing the self. I am also an energy healer for both people and animals, and a registered general and paediatric nurse. As a therapist, I am only interested in using techniques that work. Everything in this book has helped me and my clients.

When is a Good Time to Start?

A tourist asks a farmer for directions to the Grand Canyon. The farmer scratches his head, thinks for a moment then says, "If I were you, I wouldn't start from here at all." Unlike the tourist, we have to start from where we are. There is no perfect time to start the work of loving yourself unconditionally. There will never be a perfect time. There is no time to wait until the dishes are washed or the end-of-year tax return is done. This is it. Now. One of the great things about getting older is the sense of urgency that arises as the road ahead looks shorter than the one behind. We are spiritual beings in a human body, here to learn and understand. Our time in this body, this life, is finite. If you believe in reincarnation, then you may get a chance to go round again. Or not. What if this is your last lifetime? What if this is your last year in this world? Who would you spend it with? What would you do? What would you not do anymore? Would you look at the world with fresh eyes? How would your life be different? We shouldn't wait for terminal illness to strike to ask these questions and be guided by the answers.

How Will Loving Myself Improve My Life?

Loving yourself is the key to spiritual transformation. The fruit of this self-work is joy and happiness. We begin to discover that we are not isolated after all. We discover that we are, in fact, connected and have support available to us. If we choose, we can go to bed happy and wake up happy. We can laugh at the cats chasing each other in the garden, energised by the wild wind. We can have fun with our children. We can laugh at the enthusiasm of a dog running like crazy in the park. We can be grateful for making a new friend at a dance class. It is always the simple, real pleasures that bring us joy or happiness and that joy emerges from the inside out. It doesn't come with any material possession, status or trip. All those things are peripheral and fleeting. But excavating our authentic selves gives us access to great vitality and inner power. It strengthens and raises our vibrations. As that happens, our ability to attract the opportunities, people, and prosperity we desire and deserve becomes exponentially stronger. We become a magnet, bringing all these things to us through the power of our own joy and happiness.

So Loving Myself Will Solve All My Problems?

Sadly, no. But what it will do is allow you access to a goldmine of inner resources and strengths to cope with whatever life brings. When things are going well, it will allow you to feel joy. When illness, injury, loss or traumas occur (and they will because they are part of life) loving yourself helps you get through in one piece.

How Do We Become Unloving To Ourselves?

To avoid being against others, people have been taught to love others INSTEAD of themselves.
Virginia Satir, Family Therapist

There are a myriad of ways for us to lose ourselves and feel disconnected from our tribe, or our source. This can lead us to wrongly believe that we are unloved, unlovable, unsupported, unable to change and powerless. There are a million ways for us to lose our sense of self and our self-affection if indeed we ever had it in the first place. Here are a couple of them:

The Culture of Fear

The culture of fear can be acquired in childhood, through negativity in the home, school, or society in general. Children are like sponges that absorb the atmosphere surrounding them, good or bad, and the first seven years are especially crucial in terms of shaping the adult that follows.

The cultural expectations and the messages delivered through the media and the internet have an impact on us. Young girls receive damaging messages about their bodies and early exposure to sexual matters. Young boys receive messages that discourage open expression of their feelings, and that promote violence as the answer to conflict. In Western culture, there can be an absence of meaningful tribal or social ritual which marks important rites of passage as we move through life stages. This weakens our tribal connections and makes us feel isolated. It undermines our ability to see ourselves as part of a community, each with a valuable contribution to make and to benefit from the safety net of social support.

In later life, we can begin to understand how our negative conditioning has shaped us and held us back. If it happened over the course of twenty years then we might reasonably expect it to take twenty years to undo the damage and fly free. And it may. But it doesn't have to. What I've observed over the years of offering therapy is that *when a person is ready, the old patterns can dissolve quite quickly.* Awareness is what starts the process of change. It is like water dislodging a dam which then disintegrates with apparent suddenness when in actual fact it may have taken years to reach that tipping point of change and dissolution.

The Early Rocky Road - What We Need and What We Get

The family crucible shapes us. As children, we do not need perfect parenting. All we need is for it to be "good enough." Sometimes, despite the best efforts of our parents, there may be gaps in our ability to have self-respect, self-affection or self-love.

A child who is not secure in the love of a parent or guardian is vulnerable. A child who grows up in the chaos of violence, drugs, alcohol, bullying, abuse or poverty is at risk and likely to make poor choices. A child who lacks safe boundaries in childhood and teenage years is easily drawn towards alcohol and drugs as a way of trying to belong to the tribe. And we are hardwired to belong because we have the ancestral memory that to be outside the tribe equates to death.

What we missed out on – or perceive we missed out on – usually becomes our life's mission. Part of my life's mission, for instance, is comfort, due to an absence of comfort as a child. This relates to physical as well as emotional comfort. Not only do I dislike being uncomfortable myself, but I hate seeing others in discomfort as well. Sometimes this has led me to veer away from facing problems head on and therefore, as a result, prolonging them. I have had to learn to acknowledge this tendency, grasp the nettle and do what needs to be done, discomfort or not.

Roles and Masks

With work or family, we take on roles and can over identify with them. We may think that those roles are precisely who we are: parent, child, spouse, worker, and friend. We can do the activities that all these roles require but they are still not us.

Years ago, I studied drama. For one production, we were asked to make our own masks. My mask was of a bird. The eyes were deliberately set crookedly so that I would have to tip my head to one side to see out through it. In order to don the mask I had to exhale, bend my head over, put the mask on and come back upright. When you were upright, you had become the part you were playing. You inhabited the mask as if it was you. Believing that we are our roles is like wearing that mask for so long that we forget we created it ourselves. The truth is that we are much, much more than any role we play.

Dissociation

When a meteorite hit the earth and caused the end of the cretaceous period by causing an ice age, many of the plants that survived did so by encasing their precious seed in the shell of a nut for protection. In the same way, our lost selves are hidden, armoured, but still hoping to emerge and fulfil their destiny. They never give up.

In psychology, this process is called dissociation. It can be a wise strategy for the short term. In the long term, however, it causes us problems because we are missing part of our true selves.

In shamanism, it is called soul loss, the loss of power that stems from being divided from our bodies and our feelings. The lost part goes to non-ordinary reality to hide. In that non-ordinary reality, the lost soul part may not know when it is safe to return, or how to return, and that is the job of a shaman – to journey to non-ordinary reality and return with the soul fragment, through the process of soul retrieval. The lost part is then symbolically breathed into the body.

Parts of us may have gotten lost through trauma, abuse or neglect. When trauma happens, the mind can unconsciously split itself off, in the effort to try and survive. We may unconsciously disconnect our spirits from our physical bodies. As children, we are hostages to fortune; we have no choice but to physically stay where we have landed.

But our spirits have choice. Many people who have been abused describe out of body experiences, where they could see what was happening – as if it were happening to someone else. We may also zone out by getting stuck into television, computers, books, drugs or alcohol. The unconscious motto is "Anywhere but here."

Once we become aware that we are lost, the next step is to consciously decide to do something in order to feel better. If the trauma has been severe, professional help is best because otherwise it can be overwhelming. It is important to find someone trustworthy and competent to help us, someone with whom we feel safe.

The Energy Battery

When we do not love ourselves, quite often our lives are full of struggle. We are tired. Our life energy and vitality levels are low. A useful concept is the Energy Battery. It is as if we have only one Energy Battery to get us through the day. So what fills our energy battery? What drains it?

For example, the things that I have found that add to my Energy Battery are:

A good night's sleep
Daily mindfulness
Surreal humour
Daily yoga
Daily journaling
Doing things I love or playing
Fresh air and exercise
Writing
Gratitude
Sunshine
Being out in nature
Holidays
Dancing
Regular contact with supportive friends and family
Good healthy vegetarian food
Drinking plenty of filtered water
Interaction with animals
Spiritual practice
Appreciation of my health, gifts and blessings

The things that drain my Energy Battery are:

My negative thoughts and fears left unchecked
Vexatious people
The news on TV, radio, internet or newspapers
Alcohol, wheat and sugary foods
Anxiety, stress or worry
Clutter in the house
Nothing to look forward to
Too many commitments
Saying yes when I should have said no

Assessment: Where Am I Now?

There is a simple tool to let you know your starting point for your journey. It is the SUD (subjective units of distress) scale developed by Dr Joseph Wolpe in 1969.

Imagine there is a scale that goes from zero to ten. Zero represents contempt and self-hatred. Five represents some affection for the self, some acceptance of the self as it currently is. Ten represents loving the self unconditionally. Take a deep breath. Close your eyes and allow a number between zero and ten to pop into your mind. That is where you are at the moment. The goal is to gradually move as close to ten as possible.

I suggest that you keep a journal to document this journey that you have begun. It will help to show you how much progress you have made when you look back on it. So what are the things that fill or drain your Energy Battery? Write them in your journal, and then resolve to let in more of what supports you. And resolve to let go more of what drains you.

Exercise: Sit and Breathe

Breath is the bridge which connects life to consciousness, which unites your body to your thoughts.
Thich Nhat Hanh

For minor trauma, we can start the healing process by ourselves. One exercise is to choose to sit and breathe. The breath actually consists of three parts – the In Breath, the Out Breath and the tiny moment of rest between the two, which I will call the "Rest Moment." Slow the breathing down, and breathe in and out to a count of four. Once you know how long a "four" breath lasts, stop counting and just focus on the breath. Notice it going in and going out. Then pay attention to the Rest Moment. The Rest Moment is very relaxing and it slows down the rate of thoughts. It also begins to open up a healing space inside of us. This exercise is very simple and powerful. But simple does not mean easy. The ego will do its best to derail our focus. It will say things like: "This is silly. How can this help? Did I put frozen peas on the shopping list? I can't concentrate so this is not working." The trick is to continually return to the breath once we become aware we are thinking about frozen peas or whatever it might be. That is the kernel of the practice. Just stay with it, no matter what. This sitting meditation practice opens the space inside of us for our frozen hearts to thaw. With the thaw, tears may come. That's okay. Think of tears as the ice melting in our hearts. It is good to allow this process to be gradual because it prevents a storm of emotion flooding and overwhelming us. We can learn to re-parent ourselves, to calm and comfort our inner distressed selves, to re-integrate those selves with the adults we now are. This is the work. It takes as long as it takes. It is soul work. We are retrieving our own souls, no less.

Chapter 2

Making a Start

In the universe, there is an unmeasurable, indescribable force which sorcerers call INTENT, and absolutely everything that exists in the entire cosmos is attached to INTENT by a connecting link.
                                        Carlos Castaneda

Set Your Intention

In order to begin to love ourselves, we must first be aware that currently, we do not love ourselves in a healthy way. Or maybe we love ourselves a little, but not a lot, not enough. Or maybe not at all. If the title of this book resonated with you, that is an indication from your soul that more self-love is needed. Loving the self unconditionally starts by accepting the self unconditionally as we are right here, right now. Take heart: love comes on a continuum. We do not have to go from self-hatred or neglect to unconditional love in one mighty leap. We can start by forgiving ourselves for anything we perceive that we did or didn't do. From there we can begin to soften our hearts towards ourselves. We can start saying Yes to ourselves instead of always saying No. We can start allowing ourselves to receive, instead of always giving out heart energy. By doing this, we begin to learn that giving and receiving are equally important. We start being fairer with ourselves. And remember, we don't have to do it all in the one day.

The place to start the process of loving yourself in less than fifty years is with intention. The energy of intention links us to all causality and effect. Intention sets direction and is the conduit for healing and manifestation.

Setting the intention of loving yourself unconditionally lays the foundation for it to occur in actuality. When you start the work of loving yourself, the Universe opens up new ways of being in the world, new perspectives, new people, and new options to play, work and be. It is up to us to seize those opportunities, and use them so that when dying, we can look back on a life well lived, a life lived to the full.

If you are unclear about your intentions, here are three great questions to help: take your time writing the answers and remember the answers are not set in stone. What we want now will not be the same in five years' time because we will be different people then. When you set sail in a boat, you may have a destination in mind - but to stay on course requires a constant adjustment of the tiller.

1. What do you want to experience?
2. How do you want to grow?
3. How do you want to serve the world?

Once you have created your intentions, write them down, including your intention to learn how to love yourself. Sign and date the page. Commit to it. Decide that you will do whatever it takes to love yourself more in a healthy way. Focusing your attention on your intentions creates growth.

We also need to add appropriate action to the equation. For instance, if I want to sell a car, I need to set the intention of selling it, focus my attention on selling it, and take the action of advertising it in order to sell it.

Clear Intention + Attention + Appropriate Action = Positive Change.

The First Step

This is my simple religion. There is no need for temples; no need for complicated philosophy. Our own brain, our own heart is our temple; the philosophy is kindness.

His Holiness the 14th Dalai Lama

Once you have set your intentions, the first step is to decide to start being kind to yourself. If you have not directed kindness or compassion to yourself before, this can be much harder than you might expect. You must constantly select the kinder option when faced with choice. To determine the kindest option, answer this question again and again:

"If I really valued and loved myself, I would........."

Each time you make a decision to be kind and loving to yourself, you are aligning with the Divine. That's all it takes, awareness that you have a choice using free will, and then consciously deciding on being kind to yourself. It also helps to decide to become more conscious generally. When we begin to realise our own true value in our own eyes, it spurs us on to act differently and more lovingly towards ourselves. The more we do this to ourselves the more we are able to offer authentic kindness and compassion to others.

Simple kindness to one's self and all that lives is the most powerful transformational force of all.
Dr David Hawkins, Power vs. Force

We have been taught to put others before ourselves. This is a mistake. The truth is that we are equal to others. We all need kindness. To be kind to others without being kind to yourself is self-abusive. It starves you of the nurturance of love and leaves you depleted. In that depleted state, you have no authentic energy to offer others. It comes from a place of great effort. Effort and struggle are the coin of the ego. Soul living is effortless because it is the flow of unconditional love.

If we could just see, even for a moment, how amazing and perfect we are exactly as we are, even with all our imperfections, our lives would be changed forever. Our true nature is that we are Divine beings of energy and light in a physical body. Our consciousness survives beyond the body. We are sparks of Divine unconditional love.

Excavation

A shard of ancient pottery is found on the surface of the ground. It indicates that there may be hidden treasure beneath. When the archaeologist digs, she digs carefully. It is more of a brushing, a sweeping, a clearing, and a filtering process than actual digging. One excavation tool is a sieve; it allows dirt and dust to be discarded and the valuable nuggets to be identified and kept. Michelangelo worked in the same way, to "release what was already there" in the stone. He discarded the parts that did not fit the emerging creation.

We need to engage in a continual "sieving" of ourselves in order to let go of parts of ourselves or our lives that no longer fit. By doing so, we make space for our souls to emerge, blinking, into the light. We can set our intentions then, that we will be peaceful, loving, happy, joyful and abundant – but if we continually make space for growth, these are all our natural soul qualities anyway. Our work is not to add anything to ourselves, just to let go of any misperceptions about who we really are.

All we have to do is make a start. Then keep going, gently and gradually, until we emerge, gasping for breath, from the debris. We emerge into our own lives as if we had never seen them before, and indeed, for most of us – we haven't. We have never seen or been our authentic selves before. How will we know when we are arriving at our true selves? An upsurge of energy. An upsurge of enthusiasm for life. Feelings of happiness and contentment and even joy sometimes. The urge to dance, play or create. These are all signs that our souls are emerging from the darkness. This is our true divine nature. Let's party!

Growing Self Awareness through Enquiry

> *I own me and therefore, I can engineer me.*
> *I am me and I am okay.*
>
> Virginia Satir

To learn to love ourselves, we need to be in a constant state of enquiry which feeds our growing self-awareness. Here are some questions that I have found useful to ask on an ongoing basis:

Who am I?
What do I want?
What does my soul want?
How will I know when I have what my soul wants?
What did I come into this life to do or be?
How can I serve the Universe today?
What have I learned this week? This year?
How can I do things better from now on?
What will be fun and joyful for me to do or explore?
And, once again - If I really valued and loved myself, I would.........

So what are YOUR questions? Write them, and your answers in your journal.

Appreciation

A simple way to make progress in loving ourselves is the practice of self-appreciation. There will be those among you who shudder at the thought, inured as you were to steer clear of "thinking you were great" in case you "lost the run of yourself and got notions." Don't be alarmed. True self-appreciation is sincere and humble gratitude to the Creator spirit for the good being you already are. Appreciation moves you to a higher vibration. It is a higher state of being. Most of us, especially women, have at least one part of our bodies that we wish was different. This is due in part to the images of beauty portrayed in the media. In actual fact, our bodies are amazing, exactly as they are. It is usually only when we become ill or lose a body part that we begin to appreciate our good health. We take good health for granted so much of the time. But we do not have to wait until illness strikes to appreciate what we have. Answer this question: what part, system or organ of your body would you be willing to do without right now?

Appreciation Inventory

Make a list of your gifts and blessings in your journal. Include everything. The list will be long. For example, include health, (work if you have it,) family, friends, pets, a home, food, nature, holidays.......just for a start. If you have ever gone backpacking, you may have had the experience of going a long time without access to a shower, or maybe good food. I guarantee you that when you eventually got that shower or meal, you appreciated it like never before! If you are not used to thinking about the gifts you have to offer the world, ask a trusted friend to reflect them back to you. An example of a gift is being a good listener or a clear thinker. Give thanks for your gifts and blessings. This is enlightened self-interest, because whatever we focus on increases.

Exercise: Self-Appreciation

Put aside five minutes every day. Look in the mirror. Look yourself in the eye and smile. Put the first two fingers of your right hand on your heart. Repeat to yourself out loud: 'I accept myself as I am now. I like who I am. I acknowledge my needs and meet them in a kind and loving way.' There may be other truthful and kind words you need to hear out loud. Say them. Finish by saying the cheerful if ungrammatical "Well Done Me!"

Chapter 3

Making Space to Be Yourself

*The best way to run the world is to let it take its course
and to get yourself out of the way of it.*
                                                                Tao Te Ching

We have to be our own midwives as we shed the baggage to make space for our souls to grow. We are often caught up in fear of change: "I can't leave the job I hate because…the time isn't right. I might not get another one. The children are in school. I don't have the money. It's not really that bad here." The bottom line is that often we know in our hearts it is time to let go and move on, but fear stops us, so we stay put, year after year after year. We substitute the seeming comfort of the known for the uncharted waters of change. There is a cost, however. We shrink inside. Each time we put up and shut up, we shrink. We are unconsciously giving ourselves the message: this is as good as I deserve. Each time we bite back an honest response in favour of a more diplomatic one, we shrink inside. We came here for our soul to grow and expand. Expansion is our nature - and not just in the waistline as we age! When we negate that nature, we die a little inside. We shrivel.

Letting Go and Getting Out of The Way

Letting go is an integral part of healing ourselves. We carry much baggage from our past: our mistakes, our traumas, our regrets. The weight of these burdens can stop us from living in the present. There are many ways to learn to let go and it doesn't matter which of them we start to use. What matters is that we do start. Now. Today.

Because letting go is a process and we need to embed it as a habit in our lives.

Most of our major blocks are unconsciously created and maintained by ourselves. We frequently sabotage ourselves just when a great opportunity arises. Our objective is simple: to get out of our own way. To stop our unconscious fears, anxieties, misperceptions and limiting beliefs from keeping us mired in stuckness.

It's not that we need to take anything new on board to achieve this, rather that we need to set our intention to delete all obstacles to the realisation of our goals. To let go and allow. To open to receive. A dissolving of blocks as opposed to taking arms against them. We unconsciously hold on to all these fears in the vain hope of controlling our lives, but it doesn't work and all we do is hold on to the very things that keep us stuck.

There is a useful concept that comes from energy healing. If a person is sick or diseased, there are only two possibilities: either there is something inside them that is detrimental and they need to let it go, or there is something missing and they need to allow it in to nourish their hearts, minds, bodies, cells, spirits and souls.

I do quite a bit of healing work for other therapists and healers. I often say to them: "You know this already. And you know how to do this change work." They say "Yes, I do, but I can't seem to let myself do it." And that is the kernel of it. Our subconscious programming is sabotaging our apparent desire to get ahead and move along. So healing and releasing that programming is key to progress. Of course, I have my own therapist, who helps me see my blind spots and let go of my own blocks! We all need someone to help us along.

Letting go is like discovering that you have been wearing night vision goggles all your life. Your perception has been limited to less than ten per cent of your actual field of vision. When you pay attention to the process of letting go, you allow the blinkers to fall from your eyes and start seeing who you really are. At this point, you begin to realise that we are all interconnected. You start seeing that we have more in common than you may have previously thought.

Letting Go of Perfectionism

Perfectionism arises out of the need to control. It usually arises because as children, we had little or no control over our lives, or we may have gotten the message that the only way to gain approval was to make no mistakes and do everything perfectly. Perfectionism is a relentless taskmaster. The need to do things perfectly can cause us to be paralyzed with fear of making mistakes – so instead, we take no risks and do nothing. Alternatively, we may become workaholics. Perfectionism is exhausting because the goals are unachievable. Letting go of the need to be perfect is part of the journey to self-love. Acceptance of the fact that we are not perfect is the starting point of this journey. It is an allowance of the realisation that we are unique, but not special, because everyone is unique. Instead of perfectionism, we can aim for excellence. Excellence allows mistakes to be made while doing our best. It is infinitely kinder to us because it is achievable. The Pareto Principle is often used in business but can be applied to all our endeavours. In this context, it says that if we get 80% of things right, we can reasonably allow ourselves to have 20% that may be less than ideal. I like this idea: we can often achieve over 80% of course – but we are allowing ourselves the 20% room to fail, to learn from our failures. This is how we grow.

Letting Go of Mistakes and Hurts

I often tell therapy clients that the work has two parts: looking back into the past to let go and forgive, and looking to the future by aligning your intentions, thoughts and beliefs with what you want to invite into your life. When I say "work," I mean our life's work. One of my teachers, Nora O'Neill, believed that we amassed traumas in the first half of our lives so that we would have something to DO in the second half!

Sometimes we do things we regret. Other times we regret not acting or speaking out when we should have. We beat ourselves up for "what we have done," or "what we have failed to do." At other times, we have been badly hurt by others. Condemning ourselves leads nowhere. It is a closed road, one that piles guilt on top of regret.

Buying into the duality approach – this is good and that is bad, keeps us on the seesaw. It's time to step off that seesaw now and say: "That happened, it's over now, I survived and I'm all right now. I choose to learn from what happened or from what I did or didn't do. I forgive them now. I forgive myself now and I resolve to act differently and in a better way the next time."

Feng Shui: Combining Physical Action with Mental Intention

> *What makes the vessel useful is its emptiness.*
> *Tao Te Ching*

In order to become yourself (your true, authentic self, the "real you") you must let go of anything that does not reflect who you are now. You are not the same person that you were five years ago.

Using Feng Shui can help clarify who you are now. Feng Shui is the Chinese art of placement. It is also known as "clutter clearing." The Western equivalent of Feng Shui is the spring clean. Whatever you choose to call it, it is a very useful transformational tool. The reason for this is that we invest objects with symbolic meaning. I have found that asking clients to do a clear-out of clutter during therapy helps things along. Everything has a vibration and a good question to ask during this process is: Do I love this item? How do I feel about this item? If you do not love the item and/or if it makes you feel less than happy, let it go.

We can use Feng Shui to literally and symbolically release our attachments to possessions, ideas or beliefs. If we are holding on to the letter of rejection from a job thirty years ago, it can unconsciously cause us to hold on to a belief that we are not good enough.

Clearing out old photos, letters, cards or clothes can be a cathartic and symbolic act of releasing the past to make space for ourselves to expand and grow. You might choose to rearrange furniture or give some furniture away. You might choose to change how the garden looks. You have licence to be as creative as you want to be. We are making space to invite in new things and new people into our lives. It is part of getting clear on what we do want, as opposed to what we don't want. Clearing out is also an ongoing process. It is never completed until our lives are finished.

Practising Feng Shui is a way of anchoring our desire to change in our environment so that when we look at the new arrangement around us we are instantly reminded of what we are in the process of doing – letting go and getting ready for better days ahead. Letting go gives us hope for the future.

Puja: Ritual for Letting Go

A puja is a fire ceremony for symbolically releasing attachments. The reason a ritual is effective is that it is understood by the deep subconscious mind, the language of which is colour, imagery – and symbolism. The subconscious mind is extremely powerful and all change begins at a subconscious level. You might choose to safely burn that letter of rejection, for instance, to release old feelings of inadequacy or failure. Alternatively, you may choose to write down what it is you want to let go of, and burn it safely to symbolically release it.

Chapter 4

Nourishment

Mantra: *I now claim the right conditions for my mind, body, soul, heart and spirit to flourish.*

Marese Hickey

We are shaped by who we love and by our passions, the ones we pursue and the ones we deny. We have to find out what we need to nourish us, and meet that need.

Physical Nourishment

How can we be kind to our bodies now? What must we stop doing that is detrimental? What enjoyable exercise will support our physical health? What food and drink suits us best? What no longer agrees with us? Are we breathing in an optimum way? Most of us breathe in a shallow way using only the top one third of our lungs. Deep abdominal breathing triggers the relaxation response, calms us down and grounds us.

If I have a top model car which runs on unleaded petrol, I do not put diesel in it and expect it to work. And yet the highly processed foods we eat and drink are full of sugar, fat and additives which are exactly like diesel to our bodies. Sugar is especially toxic and it is only when you try to give it up you realise it is in 99% of all food products. I had occasion to go off added sugar for six weeks and I could not believe the difference in my mental clarity as a result. As the neuroscientist Candace Pert writes, "Relying on an artificial form of glucose – sugar – to give us a quick pick me up is analogous to, if not as dangerous as, shooting heroin."[2]

Honouring Our Bodies

Having good health is like having a beautiful flower in a pot. When it is in great condition, it gives us pleasure. But it needs nutrients to survive: water, good soil, sunshine, shelter from the wind. Sometimes we see a pot plant with drooping leaves and think, "I'll water that tomorrow when I have time." Then we get caught up in busyness. One day we look and it is dead. Beyond repair.

In a similar way, we ignore our own drooping vitality as our bodies try to signal to us that there is something wrong, something vital missing. Pain, physical or emotional, is always a signal that there is something amiss. What is missing is the acknowledgement that we, too, have needs that are important. The body never lies. Consistent low energy or persistent physical symptoms can, of course, be an indication of physical illness. There may be times we catch a bug and our intestines revolt, but the difference is that bodily messages recur time and time again until we heal the cause. If we go to the doctor and the pills or potions don't work, then it may be time to delve deeper. What are we trying to suppress? What is missing? What do we need to let go of? What is killing us slowly?

There are often ads for painkillers on television. The man is rowing a boat or doing a triathlon when he gets a pain. He takes the painkiller and hey presto! Pain gone, he is able to continue running or rowing. What is being ignored is that pain is a signal from the body to the mind. The message is STOP. Stop, or you will do further damage. STOP. You need to rest. If we are wise, we honour these signals. We listen and act accordingly. We remember that if we need antibiotics, we need bed rest to allow them to work properly. We respect the body-mind intelligence that knows more than we do. When our bodies are reassured that their messages are being heard, they become more cooperative and they heal faster.

When we start loving ourselves, it is as if we have to uncover layer after layer of unconscious unkindness or neglect of ourselves, including our bodies, and then make reparation. What is your body saying to you? Could you allow yourself more rest, fun, exercise or water if you needed it? If not, what would have to change in order for this to happen?

Body Signals and Feedback

*Your body is the junction
between the visible and invisible worlds.*
                                    Deepak Chopra

It is now understood that the body and mind are intimately connected. There is a saying in therapy: the issues are in the tissues. The embodiment of pleasure is health and ease, and of pain is dis-ease. The body always tells the truth. When we become aware of its messages, it can serve as an indicator of how things really are with us at this time.

If a visit to the doctor yields no answers, our bodies may be trying to tell us that something important needs to change. They may tell us through recurrent sore throats that we need to speak out. Through recurrent chest infections that there is something that we are trying to suppress, something we need to "get off our chest." Through back pain, that we feel unsupported. Through neck pain, that someone or something is giving us a "pain in the neck." Through shoulder trouble, that we are carrying too many burdens. Through difficulties on the left side of our bodies that we may need to "be" more. Through difficulties on the right side of our bodies that we may be "doing" too much. We may need to do more or do less. We may need to just be, and stop doing at all for a while. Through tension in the stomach, our bodies tell us that we are anxious. Through IBS, that the anxiety or stress is literally "giving us the runs." Through insomnia, that we have a wellspring of anxiety that emerges in the night hours and there may be something that we have to "wake up to." Any long term psychological condition that we fail to face will emerge through the body. It comes down through the auric or energy field and creates symptoms in the body.

Persistent feelings are a message from the body-mind as to the direction we need to go. For example, I once worked part-time in a company. After a couple of years, I found I was coming home on those company work days and sleeping after dinner. Then going to bed and sleeping for eight or nine hours. Eventually, I realised that working in that company was draining me, which was why I needed so much sleep. I refocused on my own work, left the company and my normal high energy returned. So the body-mind will always tell us the truth – if only we will listen. Once we hear the message, we then need to take action to change things for the better. If we do not listen, the body-mind will continue to up the ante until we are forced to listen. So it is better to act sooner rather than be forced to contend with a heart attack or stroke which our body produces to get our attention.

Emotional Nourishment

The word emotion comes from "emovere," meaning to "pass through or out." It is useful to aim to be guided by feelings but not controlled by them, because – if we allow it to happen – they will pass. They come and then they go.

We need to listen to and acknowledge our emotions. As we do this, we become more aware of what we are feeling when we are feeling it. This increases our self-awareness and moves us towards peace of mind. Nothing compensates for lack of peace of mind. No shopping trip, no shoes, no jewellery, and no car will do it.

Peace of mind, being content with who we are and our current lives – the need for this simply will not go away. Quite often there is something difficult we need to do to regain our peace of mind: it may be a conversation, a confrontation, a major change, or an exhumation of buried trauma that needs healing.

There is a balance to be struck, however, between experiencing feelings and being active. Some people have a tendency to pay a lot of attention to their negative feelings, getting stuck in a downward spiral of negativity, staying in bed and ruminating over how bad they feel. Socrates said that the unexamined life isn't worth living. He might well have added: The over-examined life isn't worth living either!

Many people deny disturbing feelings and try to ignore them or stuff them down. The problem is that they might go out of sight, but they don't go away. By denying or repressing feelings, we lose our passion for life. Once we give them space to be, they lose their power to disturb us.

By doing quality control on our own feelings, we are improving the world for others too. This is because feelings are contagious. Feelings are energy and energy is contagious. If you think about a person who is light-hearted and laughing and the way you feel cheerful when you are with them, you will recognise this as being true. Similarly, you will probably remember someone who was like a wet blanket, dampening high spirits and making everyone more serious. Or sometimes, if a friend has unloaded all their problems onto you, they go off feeling great and you feel "unaccountably" tired or headachy. Incidentally, there is a value in listening to someone's troubles – up to a point. If they come back to you a week later with the same tale of woe, however, they are likely to be just venting and may be unwilling to change. Sometimes endlessly listening to the same story is facilitating others to remain stuck. It can be useful to gently ask: 'So what are you going to do about this?' And just be quiet, and see what happens.

Exercise: Letting Go of Everyday Upsetting Emotions

Here is a technique for letting go of everyday upsetting emotions such as guilt, shame or anger. (Remember that if there is trauma involved, it is best to go to a trained therapist for help.) The next time you feel any of these emotions, try the following approach:

1. Take a deep, full breath and let it out slowly. (We often stop breathing when we feel an emotion strongly.)
2. Close your eyes.
3. Find out where in your body you are feeling the emotion. Do an internal scan, looking for tension or tightness in the head, throat, chest, abdomen, shoulders or back. These are the usual areas where strong emotions are stored.
4. Use one word to name what you are feeling, e.g. I feel it in my chest, and it is guilt.
5. On a scale of one to ten, where one is feeling okay and ten is an intense level of guilt, allow a number to arise. E.g. seven.
6. Do not judge your feeling. Simply allow yourself to feel it fully, exactly as it is.
7. Keep breathing in and out as you focus on the feeling.
8. It will start to lessen. Stay with it until it is down to level zero or one and notice how your chest feels now.
9. Now get up and move around, and do something that needs to be done. Also, drink plenty of water as releasing stuck feelings is a little like doing a body detox.

To summarise, check in with your body; name what you are feeling; allow it space without judgement, and it will be released. If there is an action your emotions are guiding you towards, take that action. Repeat this process at least once a day to release stressful or negative feelings and your life energy will increase exponentially.

Here's what you will probably notice: The minute you allow yourself to feel an emotion fully, it goes away. You can use this technique any time you feel a difficult emotion. Many of our difficulties arise because we instinctively fear the pain of feeling uncomfortable feelings. But once they are allowed to be felt, they disappear like water flowing into sand.

Spiritual Nourishment

*The things of the spirit require
careful nurture and slow growth.*

Silver Birch

Presence of the Sacred

Where in our lives is there space for sacred presence? Rushing around like lunatics, quite often our aspiration is to get through the week or even the day in one piece. We need to set time aside to slow down and sit. To realise that we are human beings, not human doings. There is a Gary Larson cartoon, of a cow guru in a Buddhist saffron robe. Another cow disciple sits at her feet. The guru instructs the disciple: "And remember to slow down and eat the roses on the way!" Whether we choose to smell the roses or eat them, we need to make time to at least notice them. We need stillness and quietness. Only in stillness can we begin to appreciate the beauty of our inner and outer worlds. When I say the word 'sacred,' I am talking about our own personal connection with our Creator, however, we might perceive that. For me, sacred space can be a grove of spruce trees in the local park or it can be an internal, portable experience. I always intentionally set up sacred space in my therapy room before a healing session with a human or animal client. Included in my definition of sacred space are the occasions when we do our soul work. For example, each week I volunteer as an animal healer in Dog's Aid rescue centre. When I am with the animals, just me and them, offering them healing or playing with them, time disappears. I emerge from those hours recharged. The practice benefits me at least as much as them! I am completely relaxed and present in the moment with them. To me, that is also the presence of the sacred, the allowing of my true inner self to come forward.

What defines your sacred space? Create for yourself a mini altar to anchor your intention to love yourself, and each time you see it your subconscious mind will be inspired to magnetise what your soul needs for your journey at this time.

In order to grow spiritually, we need time for self-reflection, calmness, stillness and the space to expand. We need to claim this for ourselves despite the clamour for attention of family, friends, phones and the myriad other distractions. We also need to play.

Becoming aware of our own needs is the next step. If an angel were to appear beside you now and offer you whatever you want, what would you ask for – for yourself? (Not for someone else in your life.) Is it a walk, a trip to the library, a coffee with your best friend? Listen and then act on what emerges.

These things are not a waste of time. They are nurturing for the spirit and soul. We need to feed our spirit to inspire our soul to emerge. Our true selves are in there, waiting patiently for us to open the door and let them out.

Good Questions

What is the highest vision you can have for yourself?

What do you want written as your obituary when you pass into spirit?

How can you be kind to yourself today?

How can you be kind to other humans today?

How can you be kind to animals or the environment today?

What action could you take that is in alignment with your deepest values?

Could you start using only cosmetics that are not tested on animals?

Could you cycle or walk instead of using the car, thereby reducing pollution?

For some, prayer, meditation or mindfulness is the daily balm for the soul that fertilises growth. For others, it is a walk by the sea or in the woods. All that matters is that we are aware of this aspect of ourselves and regularly find a way to honour it in a way that works for us.

It takes constant awareness to keep growing but once you start, there is no turning back. As Hakim Sanai says, "When the path ignites a soul, there's no remaining in place."

Mental Nourishment

*Life consists not only of the things we do
but of the things we say and the things we think.*
Silver Birch

Words that Shape Your Life

We have no problem believing the World Wide Web connects us all via the Internet even though we can't see it. Our human energy connections are just as real even though they, too, are invisible. Energy follows thought. An important part of learning to love ourselves depends on becoming more aware of our thoughts. That includes the thoughts we have about ourselves, and about others. Our thoughts create our reality, and can have a physiological effect on others besides ourselves.

Controlling the Subconscious Powerhouse

Positive thoughts have a profound effect on behaviour and genes but only when they are in harmony with subconscious programming.
Bruce Lipton, Cellular Biologist

All change starts at a subconscious level. Ninety five percent of our behaviour is controlled by our subconscious minds running on automatic programs that were taken on board before we were seven years old. That includes the experience of the foetus in the womb during gestation as it was flooded with the same hormones as the mother – for good or bad. From two to six years of age, the brain waves operate mostly at the theta wave level of 4-8 Hz which is the suggestible state used in hypnosis. When there is a conflict between the conscious mind (willpower) and the subconscious mind (imagination), the subconscious mind will always win out. Whatever is happening or not happening in our lives is due to our subconscious beliefs. That is why it is vital to make sure that our conscious intentions and our subconscious programs are in sync. When they are, we are powerful agents of change.

The subconscious mind is extremely powerful – and it is also like a five year old child. It is much better for us to be in charge of it, rather than having it running the show. Otherwise, it is like being in the supermarket with a five year old child and allowing the child to throw whatever it likes into the trolley. We would end up with a lot of unwanted goods and little or nothing to eat for the next week!

The language that the subconscious mind understands is imagination, colour, images, music and symbolism. That is why there are visualisation exercises and symbolic rituals included in this book because they speak directly to the subconscious mind and, therefore, accelerate the pace of positive change.

The subconscious mind also has no filter and no sense of humour. Whatever we repeat to ourselves regularly is accepted by it without question, good or bad. It takes us literally and does not understand the words "no" or "don't." So if you constantly say to yourself, "I <u>don't</u> want to be alone," what it hears is: "I want to be alone." And because it is so powerful, it manifests aloneness. In contrast, "I am lovingly connected," is a positively framed command or affirmation understood by the subconscious mind. When such a command is frequently repeated, the subconscious mind understands this to be your desire and manifests it. This command must, of course, be allied to taking action to connect you with others such as interaction through work or play. So we must be very careful what we are thinking and how we are phrasing our thoughts.

An example of this happened to me years ago, long before I knew about how the mind works. I had left school and was adrift in unemployment. I reviewed the available training options at the time and I remember thinking, "Whatever I do, I *don't* want to be a nurse." I repeated this frequently. I inadvertently focused on what I did NOT want. And guess what I became? That's right, a nurse!

The trick is to focus on what you DO want, not on what you don't want. This is where affirmations are very useful. Affirmations are like having a healthy dinner in the freezer so that when you come home from work, tired and hungry, you have something nourishing to eat that is already prepared. Otherwise, you may end up eating junk. Most of the thoughts we think are junk unless we consciously direct the mind in a positive way. It is vital to repeat affirmations to ourselves when we are feeling good – if we wait until things go wrong, the mind will revert to its default negatives. Affirmations are powerful, positive statements that can replace the negativity in your mind when repeated regularly. "I am becoming more kind to myself every day now," or "I am open now to my highest good" or "I now choose to be calm and peaceful," are examples. It is even better to create your own affirmations that suit your situation best.

The words we use to ourselves in our inner thoughts shape our reality. So what words nourish our wellbeing? What words and thoughts bring us down? If we focus on only negative thoughts, we create negativity and stress in our lives. If we practise focusing on gratitude, appreciation and positive thoughts, we create positive opportunities and relationships.

Becoming aware of our negative thoughts towards ourselves is the first step in letting them go. So when I make a mistake, I have learned to say to myself, "Well, it's irritating, but not life threatening." Over time, with this practice, we lay down new neural pathways and we become kinder to ourselves. Humour returns to us when difficulties arise. Perspective helps: a good question to ask is – how important will this be in one year's time?

A long time ago there was a saying about using computers: garbage in, garbage out. It is wise to become more discerning about what we allow into our mental space. Think about what is on the news. It's all negative, fear-based bad news which brings your energy down. That's why a "news fast" is a good idea. It's like a brain detox. Give yourself permission to stop listening to the news and reading newspapers for a month or permanently.

The feelings we feel are created and fed by the thoughts we think. Energy follows thought. And whatever we focus our attention on grows. When you focus your attention, it causes a mental state to occur. When this state is repeatedly created, it causes a trait to emerge and it literally changes the brain by causing increased myelin sheath and synaptic growth. How amazing is that! But notice the word *repeatedly*. It takes a minimum of sixteen to thirty consecutive days of repeating a new behaviour in order to embed it as an ongoing habit in our lives. Reprogramming the subconscious mind can be done through hypnosis, mindfulness (which makes us more conscious of our thoughts and, therefore, more able to change them), repetition leading to new habits, and energy psychology techniques such as the Emotional Freedom Technique (also known as EFT or tapping.) See the Resources section for more information on EFT.

Good Questions

What thoughts support me on my journey now?

Which ones are spam/junk?

What are the highest and best thoughts I can think about myself and others?

Please note that the following visualisation and all the subsequent meditations are available for download. See the Resources page for details.

Visualisation: Discovering the Treasure Within

Make yourself comfortable. Take a deep breath in and as you breathe out, allow your eyes to close. Focus your attention on your breathing. As you breathe in, imagine you are breathing in deep relaxation. As you breathe out, you are beginning to let go. Soften the eyes, the chest, and the belly.

As you go deeper inside, you approach a sacred place where there is a treasure. That treasure is your true self. Your true self is peaceful and harmonious. Your true self has a treasure trove of resources. These include your ability to see, hear, touch, taste, smell, feel, think, move, speak and choose - the ability to accept all parts of yourself, to respect and appreciate all your good parts, and to lovingly change what you wish to change. Realise how rich in resources you already are. These inner resources have already helped you through hard times in the past. In your deep sacred space, you understand at a deep level that you are much more than any hurt or trauma of the past. You understand that you are much more than your fears or your story. You are whole, exactly as you are right now. You are enough, exactly as you are right now. You are powerful because you are capable of change. You are powerful because you receive healing energy from the centre of the earth which grounds you and helps you manifest what you want and need. You are powerful because you receive healing energy from the heavens, which inspires you creatively and intuitively. You are powerful because whatever happens, you know your true self can handle it. Remind yourself that you are free to choose what fits you best now. You are free to clearly say "yes" to what fits you and "no" to what does not. You find it easy to incorporate more and more of your rich inner resources in your daily life from this moment onwards, as you slowly and gently return to the everyday world.

Chapter 5

Recovering Your Power

*Mastering others is strength,
mastering yourself is true power.*

Lao-Tzu

Waiting for the Prince on a White Horse

In the fairy-tale, the prince sweeps in on his white horse and carries the heroine off to happy ever after. That story is corrosive because it propagates the myth that the source of power is external to us. That a mysterious "something" will happen to change things for the better. That another person will come and do the work for us; that they will pick up the phone and have the difficult conversation that we are avoiding; that they will put pen to paper to apply for the new job, or write the letter of resignation to the job that is killing our soul. That another person will somehow reassure us that it will all work out. Alas, I have bad news. There is no knight on a white steed coming to make it all better. There is no happy ever after without daily work and commitment. There is no such external person or power. No-one is going to instigate the changes if we do not.

There is no real reassurance because we have to take a risk and just trust ourselves to find our way, come what may. The power is in us, plain and simple. We either take responsibility for our lives and everything in them or we crash around doing the headless chicken dance. It is not easy to take responsibility, but it gets easier the more you do it.

A useful affirmation for recovering your power is:

I cope well now with all life brings to me.

Blame versus Responsibility

> *It's not our genes but our beliefs
> that control our lives.*
> Bruce Lipton Ph.D., Cellular Biologist

When I hear someone blaming another person for something, I know that the one doing the blaming feels powerless. We give away our power when we place too much dependence on the external world or on other people. We also become powerless when we speak negatively of ourselves, whether internally or out loud.

If I say "He made me feel angry," I am giving my power to the one who allegedly made me feel angry. In truth, no-one can make me feel anything I do not choose to feel. Regardless of the circumstances, I can take responsibility for how I feel, and by taking responsibility, I take back my power. Other people are going to do what they are going to do. We have no control over that. We only have full control over what we ourselves do and how we react.

Some people blame "The System." The system is as it is. Undoubtedly there is unfairness. The system may change eventually – but our lives could be over before that happens if it happens at all. There is no-one "out there" to blame. Some people devote their lives and even give their lives to change an unfair system. Martin Luther King was an example. He was a powerful agent of change. It is also useful to consider our expectations because we are only disappointed when our expectations are unrealistic. As Lama Yeshe says, "If you expect your life to be up and down, your life will be much more peaceful."

So there may be external obstacles, but we have full responsibility – and power – over our reactions to those obstacles, people or stressors. The buck stops here. That is a powerful stance.

Epigenetics is part of what is termed "New Science," which unites science and spirituality. It was thought for years that our genes determined large parts of our lives – our tendency towards a certain familial illness, for example. However, research in cellular biology by Bruce Lipton[3] among others has shown that our beliefs switch on or off our genes. We can control what genes are operational by what we choose to believe. A belief is just an idea we think over and over until we start thinking that it is true. Then we start acting like it is true. Then it becomes true. The awareness of the effect of our thoughts/beliefs on our biochemistry should point to the obvious: control our thoughts, control our lives.

When we focus our attention on what we can do, be or have (as opposed to what we cannot do, be or have) we immediately start to regain our power. This includes taking responsibility for our thoughts and actions. When we take responsibility for everything in our lives, there is no one left to blame. It's all up to us. Scary – but powerful!

Once we take responsibility for our lives, we start empowering ourselves. With our own power available to us, we can change our lives for the better. When we change our own lives, we unconsciously give permission to those connected to us to change theirs. Alternatively, our changes may make them uncomfortable and conflict or partings may ensue. We cannot afford to let our own fears or the fears of others hold us back from bringing our truth and light to the world. Life is too short.

Life Review

In order to let go of the past, we need to acknowledge what happened in the past that was difficult, painful or hurtful. Acknowledging the truth has value in itself. It frees up the huge amount of life energy tied up in denial. As we work on loving ourselves, we find ourselves drawn to what is true and authentic, like bees to nectar. Being true to ourselves gives us new self-respect and increases our vitality. We become stronger.

We can begin by acknowledging that our pain exists and that it is real. We need to find a trusted person to whom we can Say the Words Out Loud: "This happened to me, I did this, or this was done to me." I couldn't tell you how many therapy clients have said to me, "I never told anyone about that before now." As they leave, they tell me they are feeling lighter inside. It's not that I am the right therapist for everyone, just that I am the right therapist for those who come to me. This is because I always set the intention that "only those clients who are enlightened by my work and energy come to me now." They have sent out the cry for help to the Universe and they find their way to my door. We need to urgently address the pain in our lives so that we can begin to live more fully and bring more light, happiness, creativity, peace and joy into the world. That is important, because in changing ourselves, we literally change the world.

Forgiveness

Forgiveness is releasing ourselves from the hurt of the past so that we may move on with our lives. Forgiveness is not condoning the wrong that was done. That wrong may have been done to you, by you or to yourself. It may have been intentional or unintentional. Often we create elaborate stories about how we were wronged. Holding on to these stories drains our Energy Battery and serves no soul purpose. We are all here to learn. We all make mistakes. And making mistakes is often how we learn.

Judging others and being unable to forgive them is understandable but unwise. If you have been hurt by another, the person who hurt you may not know or care that they hurt you. It is extremely likely that they are not carrying guilt over the event. It is just you that is holding on to it, carrying that heavy burden and holding yourself back. You are the one who is hurting, not them. In energetic terms, any unforgiven issues sit in your energy field and act as a magnet for more of the same. Forgiveness cleanses and heals your aura. It is about letting go so that we may be free.

There are many ways to begin the work of forgiving. One way is to write a list of those people who hurt you in the past. Visualise each one and say to them: I forgive you. Then work on the list of people you may have hurt, intentionally or unintentionally, in the past. From your heart, ask their forgiveness. Where possible, make reparation. Then let go. Then turn your attention to yourself. Think of the ways in which you have harmed yourself, your body, your spirit. Think of the pollutants or the negative mind-set. Ask forgiveness from your own self. Allow it to happen. When you are finished, safely burn the lists and let it all go. The ritual of burning is a symbolic act of release. It allows you to travel more lightly.

Exercise: Forgiveness

This exercise can be used to forgive others, but if there has been major trauma, or if there is a person you can't forgive, then it may be wise to seek external help from a therapist or counsellor to help you process the healing safely.

Turn the phone off and make yourself comfortable. Take a deep breath in and as you breathe out, relax and let go. Allow yourself to continue breathing in and out until you become quiet inside. Imagine you are in a room sitting at a plain table. There is a protective screen in front of you. You can see the person you want to forgive is sitting at the other side of the table, but you realise that you are completely safe. Look them in the eye and speak from the heart to them. You can do this silently. Say what needs to be said to unburden your heart. Then imagine that you become the other person and sit at the other side of the table. You are now looking at yourself through their eyes. If they have something to say, say it now. Then become yourself again. Repeat the process until everything is said. Then imagine you both stand up. Imagine there are dark energy cords connecting you to this person. Visualise the Archangel Michael cutting all those cords with his sword of blue light. The cords are taken up into the Violet Flame for instant transformation and release. You move the other person to a distance that is safe and healthy for you. Take as much time as you need to process the healing that has taken place, and in your own time, open your eyes and come back to full awareness, feeling lighter inside.

Chapter 6

Releasing Fear

I took refuge in silence. So fearful of saying the wrong thing, I saw words as the most powerful thing in the world, never to be uttered without deep considered thought. My mother could kill with a word and was nearly as good with a look. I worked hard to compose my face so that my thoughts were also hidden. By the time I was twelve these habits mostly ensured I remained invisible and safe.
Grow: Soul Survivors, Vol. 3

People who grew up in a rigid family system with harsh rules and poor communication naturally have low self-worth. Others fared all right at home but faced a brutal regime at school. Whatever the source, fear, guilt, lack of self-belief, poor boundaries and perfectionism are just some of the ways in which lack of self-love can manifest.

Children instinctively understand that no matter what madness a parent or guardian may display, their survival depends on them. To lose them is death. So we do what we have to do to survive. When we become adults, our habits stay with us. These habits are all based on fear. We fear being seen at all. More precisely, we fear our real selves being seen, as it was never safe to allow such vulnerability in the past. As we embark on a journey of releasing baggage, we begin to realise that habits that once worked for us are now working against us.

In the work of reshaping our lives, the bottom line is the need to feel safe. We may never have felt safe, or it may have been an infrequent experience. One way to start overcoming fear is by using affirmations, which are powerful present-tense statements of intent. The phrase "I am becoming..." is useful because once you intend growth to happen, it does. Therefore, to state that you are becoming a certain way is true. It may be an infinitesimal growth each day, or it may be a quantum leap, but, either way, it is true. And it is very important to only state things to ourselves that are true. We are hardwired to need truth for survival. If I want to cross a busy road, I need to look both ways to assess the oncoming traffic. I need to see what is real and what is right in front of me, or I will get killed. "I am becoming safer every day now," is a positive way to start feeling safer moment by moment, day by day. It then becomes a self-fulfilling prophecy.

In the work of letting down defences, we must be gentle with ourselves. Practising being more open with someone we already trust would be wise. Practising mindfulness calms the self in the time of transition. To commit to sitting down each day, and just allowing ourselves to be as we are, is in itself a transformative practice.

Overcoming Negativity

How do we restore equilibrium when life gets us down? When there is a pile up of challenges and we feel dispirited? On a physical level, this is a good time to pay attention to self-care, eating good quality food and taking exercise to release stress and ground us. When we are stressed, we become dehydrated. When the body issues a dehydration alert, more stress hormones are released into the system, making things worse. So making sure we are well hydrated is always a good idea. Taking a break and doing even a ten minute walk has positive psychological effects which last for two hours afterwards. Doing deep abdominal breathing during that ten minute walk doubles the benefit because during times of stress we tend to use only the top one third of our lungs, which worsens the stress. Deep abdominal breaths reverse this, releasing the relaxation response which cancels out the stress response.

Another avenue to explore is to be aware of our thoughts. When we feel negative, we are thinking negative thoughts, which close us off from many options. Kinesiology is a complementary therapy that uses muscle testing to identify and correct physical, emotional or spiritual imbalances. John Diamond, an Australian psychiatrist and kinesiologist, talks about the "homing thought." This is a thought that summarises our purpose in life, and it can overcome any negative influence, idea or situation. For example, my personal homing thought is: I was born to be a healer, writer and animal helper. What is your homing thought? Write it down and practise using it so that it is at the ready when you need it most.

Challenging the Inner Critic

*Keep your thoughts positive
because your thoughts become your words.
Keep your words positive
because your words become your behaviour.
Keep your behaviour positive
because your behaviour becomes your habits.
Keep your habits positive
because your habits become your values.
Keep your values positive
because your values become your destiny.*

Gandhi

It is estimated that we have over 60,000 thoughts every day. Ninety percent of them are the same as the ones we had yesterday. Many of them are negative. A belief is a thought that we continued thinking until we started thinking it was true. Once we believed it to be true, our perceptual filter eliminated all evidence to the contrary. Then we started acting like it was true. This is how people believed that the world was flat. They believed it, and they thought Columbus was going to fall off the edge of the world. So a belief can feel true, and seem true – and still be false. Beliefs are the framework for our lives so it is important that we choose beliefs that allow us to live our best lives to the fullest.

It's important to know ourselves well enough to identify the beliefs that are running our lives – the ones that work for us, and the ones that work against us. How can we advance our self-knowledge? By looking at where our lives are stuck or not working. This will indicate to us any useless beliefs that need to be changed to improve our lives. Our beliefs form a framework for our lives. My Dad used to say about me as a joke that I was "as free from money as a frog from feathers!" We both laughed because it was true, or seemed true at that time. I loved my Dad, and therefore, I subconsciously took this joke on board, because the subconscious mind has no sense of humour and accepts exactly what we put in there without discrimination. The subconscious mind has logic of its own, and it believed that in order for me to continue to be loved and approved of by him, I had to stay free of money. And I did, until I began to understand that for me to be constantly broke was not his intention or desire for me. And it was not what I wanted any more either. So I changed my belief about money being scarce, and my finances changed for the better as a reflection of that new belief.

So how do we go about changing our beliefs? Awareness of what we are thinking is the first step. Then making a decision on a moment by moment basis to choose or create thoughts that are positive. Once we do this often enough, a new neural pathway is laid down for this new habit of thinking positively. When a negative thought creeps in, as it will, just think "Cancel, cancel," and focus on what you DO actually want to happen. There is no quick fix to create a habit of thinking positively, but if we have become stuck in a cycle of negative thought, then an energy medicine tool such as Emotional Freedom Therapy (see EFT in Resources section) is very useful for getting us back on track.

Being careful with your thoughts can lead to interesting experiences. For example, years ago I directed my thoughts carefully and visualised a trip to Tibet. I imagined everything in great detail, with the flights connecting and all going well. Here is what happened on the actual trip: The flight to China had a tailwind and arrived in Beijing an hour early. Despite being unable to speak Chinese, I was able to change my onward connecting flight to an earlier one. When I arrived in Chengdu, where I was to catch the flight to Tibet, I was wandering around lost, looking for my hotel. Despite having no map, I looked up suddenly and there it was! The next morning I went out of the front door of the hotel and a hundred metres away was the only travel agency in the city that sold airline tickets to Tibet. (This was in the days before the Internet.) I made friends on that trip that lasted for years. And on it went, everything just dropping into place, easily and effortlessly, even better than I had imagined it.

Usually, however, we unwittingly allow our thoughts to work against us. We can be so harsh on ourselves. I often ask clients to say out loud a common negative phrase that they say to themselves. Mostly they won't. I ask: would you say that to your child? Your best friend? No. But we can be relentlessly critical and self-denigrating. It is because we have internalised the critical voices we heard outside ourselves as children. As adults, we now understand – intellectually – that such phrases and words are not to be used with those we cherish. As adults, we know that the old nursery rhyme that "sticks and stones will break your bones but words will never hurt you" is wrong. Words can indeed hurt you, and go on hurting all your life until you heal that hurt. So we silently use these harsh pronouncements on ourselves. As children, we may have been "brought down a peg or two" by adults. One of my secondary school teachers informed the entire class that we would never amount to anything and would be lucky if we got work in a bean factory!

The voice of the inner critic is also the voice of the ego. It is always fearful, negative, separatist and pessimistic. It always contracts us as opposed to expanding us. It sounds authoritative but is based on fear. With practice, it can be redirected to produce a kinder and more useful running commentary. We now know that our invisible thoughts, feelings and beliefs shape our visible world. As the physicist David Bohm says, "We live in a universe that is both visible and invisible."

So our external reality is only limited by our capacity to understand who we really are and then act accordingly. Sounds simple! And like many vital concepts, it is simple, but simple doesn't mean easy.

Imagination and Self-Talk

We see the world not as it is, but as we are.
Arthur Schopenhauer

To change our external world, we need to refashion our inner landscape first. Our self-talk mirrors our imagination. In a battle between imagination and will power, imagination always wins. When we keep our self-talk positive, the highest desires that we have consistently imagined manifest, when teamed up with appropriate action. Self-talk is frequently anything but logical. If I believe that "Nothing ever works out for me," even if there are exceptions showing evidence to the contrary, these are discounted to fit in with my existing perceptual filter that.....nothing ever works out for me! Using problem-solving, rational, critical thinking to "solve" why you feel a certain way just does not work.

The mind will always spew out negative self-talk and judgemental thinking which separates us from others. There is no point in trying to stop it doing what it does.

Left to its own devices, the mind will think anything! But we can step off the treadmill by mindful awareness of the present moment. This brings us back to the here-and-now.

The Stop Light Technique

One technique for bringing us back to the present moment is the Stop Light. Imagine a red traffic light. Each time you find yourself in a negative tailspin, imagine a Stop Light. Then redirect your attention to everyday items around you. Name them, out loud if you are alone, and silently if not. "Washing machine, fridge, cooker, cat etc." What this does is bring you back into awareness of the present moment. In the present moment, you can choose to focus your attention on more useful thoughts such as "I am relaxing now. I am beginning to feel better now. I am becoming calmer now."

When we are future focused, we are usually anxious. When we are past-focused, we are usually feeling sad or stuck. In the here and now, we take back the reins of control from our ego. And that feels better.

In the Now, things may be okay. Or not. But at least, they are real, unlike the scary scenarios thrown up by the ego. When my father was terminally ill, I tried to be mindful. When I said to myself, "In this moment, all is well" I instantly thought, "That's a lie. Things are not well at all in this moment." It is important to say only true things to ourselves. So instead, I chose to think: "In this moment, things are as they are." And THAT was true. And it brought me a little closer to acceptance of how things really were. In that acceptance, some small comfort was to be had.

Recognising Truth

Be hungry for truth.

Marese Hickey

When trying to identify what is true for us, a useful barometer is to notice what is happening inside us, to notice the energy vibration involved and ask: Does this feel light or heavy? Constrictive or expansive? The lighter and more expansive option is the one that is in line with our internal values. This is also a means of tuning into our own internal experience, and finding out what is right for us. It increases our trust in ourselves to be able to answer our own questions.

Acknowledging the truth of who we really are unleashes a torrent of vitality in us. To find out who we really are, all we need to do is choose. Choose what *we* want, honour ourselves first. In doing so, we can offer our authentic vital selves to the world and offer a model to others of how to be healthy, happy and the real deal. That is why loving ourselves first is not selfish but is actually of benefit to everyone in our lives.

Words can have resonance for us too. They can help to heal us. When they resonate with you they may bring tears of recognition to your eyes. This is innate recognition of something that is true for you. If this happens to you, notice carefully what the words are, and what that truth is, because it is something your soul is crying out for. Someone says something kind at the right time and it goes straight to the soul. Sometimes we are starved of the truth for so long that hearing or reading the truth can be like arriving at an oasis in the desert: we drink greedily, needing to replenish our dying souls. When you begin the journey to loving yourself, beware! Anything in your life that is not truthful or does not match your ever-increasing vibration will have to go. It can be painful to let go. But it is necessary. This is the work of the heart. It is like pruning a thorny rose bush hard in autumn, getting down to what is still vital and alive, cutting out dead wood so that come summer, there will be an abundance of blooms. You may bleed in the pruning but you will recover and be the stronger for it. The fruit of letting go is increased strength of purpose and clarity of vision.

Visualisation: The Safe Place

Switch off the phone and make yourself comfortable. Take a deep breath in and as you breathe out, allow your eyes to close. Focus your attention on your breathing. As you breathe in, imagine you are breathing in deep relaxation. As you breathe out, you are beginning to let go. Soften the eyes, the chest, and the belly. Let the shoulders drop as if you are leaving down your burdens. Imagine that there is a gateway that leads into your safe place which is surrounded by a protective shield. Open the gate and go on through. Close the gate behind you. Allow your safe place to be as beautiful as possible, a place that fills your soul and soothes your spirit. Allow yourself to notice what it looks like, the colours....what it sounds like...use all your senses....but especially notice how good it feels. Take your time. Now capture all of the elements of your safe place by bringing finger and thumb together on one hand. From now on, you find yourself making that finger and thumb gesture, at least a hundred times a day, consciously and unconsciously. Each time you do, it releases within you these same feelings of being safe and protected at all times. These feelings grow stronger within you with every hour of every day that goes by from this moment onwards. The safer you feel, the more you relax and allow your life to improve in a way that is meaningful for you. As you open your heart, you allow it to heal. As you heal your own heart, you help the ancestors and others in your life to heal their hearts too. When you choose to open your eyes, you return to the everyday world feeling safe, relaxed, open and free.

Chapter 7

Light hearted and Light footed

> *"Can you remember any of your past lives?"*
> *"At my age, I have a problem remembering what happened yesterday."*
>   Interviewer and the 14th Dalai Lama

The Power of Humour and Play

Another way of beginning to heal ourselves is through play. Many of us adults had a "rocky ride" through childhood and as a result missed out on playing. We were too busy working, or caretaking, or trying to survive, to simply play. We were too worried or stressed or too hungry to just play. So it can be healing, as an adult, to begin simple activities that invite our inner child to relax and open up to a new way of being in the world. The ego ignores play because it is "only play." But play can be a powerful healing force. It is always extremely relaxing to do an activity where we lose track of time, and any right-brain activity will do that for us. In losing track of time, we begin to regain lost parts of ourselves. Any pleasurable, creative activity that we enjoy is innately healing. Whether it is painting, drawing, knitting or making candles, it doesn't matter. What matters is that firstly, we are willing to give ourselves time to do it and secondly, that we give ourselves permission. This permission may not have been granted to us as children but as adults, we can claim back our power. No-one will hand us this time unless we claim it as our own. By taking such time to play we are giving our subconscious minds the message that we are safe now, and that we value ourselves enough to meet our own needs.

Life is too important to be taken seriously.
Oscar Wilde

Taking ourselves too seriously means we have lost perspective. Think of great leaders like the fourteenth Dalai Lama who is always smiling. He has plenty to despair about, given the state of his native Tibet, and yet his hallmark approach is humour, kindness and lightness. Mandela was known for his willingness to dance well into his old age, despite twenty seven years in prison and the challenges of his emerging South African nation. Archbishop Desmond Tutu is a man with a lot to say, but also with a huge and ready smile.

Our pets are a great help to keep us grounded and lighten our hearts for us on bad days. As I write this at the kitchen table, Felicity Sophia, my youngest cat, interrupts me by walking over the jotter, leaping into the middle of a plant and sticking her paws into the small fountain on the table. She wants to play and she is right. Play is the work of the soul.

We are never too old to play or tell good stories to lighten the load. My writing buddy who is in her seventies told me a story about her sister when they were young. Their older brother pushed the sister into a bunch of nettles. Unwilling to let him have the upper hand, her sister shouted: "I was jumping into them anyway!" Now that's the spirit!

Healing Through Dance and Movement

The therapeutic value of dance is well established as a means of raising the spirit and healing the spirit too. The combination of music, movement and social interaction is healing for us at all levels. A fascinating means of reuniting us with our lost selves is Biodanza. It was created by Rolando Toro, a Chilean psychiatrist and anthropologist. Finding the psychiatric model inadequate, he started experimenting by having music for patients in his sitting room. Biodanza has become a worldwide therapeutic force from those humble beginnings. It is healing, transformative, gentle, kind and fun. It is creative dance to mostly Latin music. Through dance and movement, we begin to explore our physical bodies and how they express our communication with self and others. It allows us to non-verbally embody our intent. Because of this, we bypass the internal censor and make progress. We bypass our own resistance and get out of our own way. It is similar to the Jungian concept of taking a symbol from a dream and putting a representation of it into our physical environment, to anchor the meaning of that symbol in our reality and in doing so, bring what it represents into being. It is alchemy at its best. For me, Biodanza has been a revelation. The words and themes used resonate with me: tenderness, potential, flying, integration, determination, love for self, love for humanity, compassion. When I started doing Biodanza, I was shocked to discover how difficult it was for me to look another person directly in the eyes. This was a reflection of my low self-esteem at the time. I learned how to reconnect with my body, and in doing so, knit my mind and spirit back into the garment of myself. Biodanza allows us to express our need to interact as social beings in a respectful and kind way, learning to make eye contact if we have been cast down, learning how to respectfully hold the hand of another. We need integration with ourselves but we also need interaction with others.

Seven months of Biodanza later, I had made major life changes and I felt much better about myself. The theme of this class was "Liberating the Inner Child." In one exercise, we formed groups to pretend to collect food and bring it to a central point in the room. Then we "lit a fire" and "went to sleep" as a group around it, having gentle physical contact with each other as we lay there. Lying in the communal space touched a place of great loss inside me. It was grief for the absence of the simple pleasures of play and safe rest. It was grief for the absence of belonging.

I realised that this loss was not about remembering childhood games nostalgically but instead becoming aware of what I never had. The experience explained to me instantly and non-verbally what psychological theories had not: that even though there had been huge gaps in my experience as a child, as an adult it is possible to fill in those gaps, to reconnect, to learn how to play, how to be with others in a safe way. It brought the theory down from the head into the body and I understood at last that I was truly not alone.

We need to be physically touched in a kind way. It has been well documented that children who lack physical contact grow into emotionally crippled adults even when their basic needs have been met. Of course, the ultimate quest is for us to have our own loving partner, with whom we share a bond of trust, affection and positive physical contact. But many people don't have that; how then are their needs for physical affection met? Even a hug from a friend will do – research has shown that twelve hugs a day lower the blood pressure! Companion animals can also have a vital role in keeping us healthy and sane. A London hospital found that children who had been abused could not be emotionally reached by staff – but could connect emotionally with small animals, such as rabbits. That was their way back to the fold. In meeting our own needs, we are better able to then reach out and help others.

Dancing, with the combination of social interaction and music, (I'm not talking about techno beat in a nightclub here!) has proven to be beneficial on a physical and psychological level. Moderate exercise is defined as one hour three days per week. Dr Daniel Siegel regularly prescribes aerobic exercise four to five times per week to reduce depression. He actually writes it on his prescription pad and hands it to his patients. Nelson

Mandela was a great man for dancing, or as the saying goes, for "Shaking the Wicked Hoof!" So let your spirit sing through your body and play with the moon.

Drumming and Resonance

When I attended my first drumming circle, I had no idea what to expect. The teacher taught three different rhythms and then split us into three groups. While one group practised, the other groups waited in silence. I was amazed to find that when another section of the group was drumming, there was an actual answering vibration or resonance in my drum even as it sat between my knees, with my hands still. It is one thing to talk about resonance and a completely different thing to experience it physically. In the centre of the room, a circular tray of candles had been set up to provide a focal point. When the three section rhythm was established, the lights went down and there we were, the tribe drumming around the fire.

I noticed that if I missed a beat, it went unnoticed in the group. I could wait and join in again when I got the rhythm back. The music was literally entrancing, and because of that, even though it was noisy, it was extremely relaxing. People left one rhythm section and took a rest in the centre of the circle, or joined another section. It was all very fluid and easy, like one large body functioning as a whole. It was restorative, connecting, healing. At the end, we observed a moment of silence to allow the sound to be absorbed. The silence was deafening after the noise of thirty five drums going for two hours. The teacher sounded a singing bowl once. It was the perfect balance. We all stood and gathered around the "fire", scooped healing energy up from the ground and sent it to each other and the Universe. What a healing experience to have the combination of connection with people, music making (even for the tone-deaf like me!), sound healing through vibration, and fun! Wonderful.

Your Challenge

Allow yourself to focus on what makes you laugh. It might be a good friend that you need to meet for a coffee and chat or a night out dancing. It might be going to a comedy show with a friend. How can you bring more laughter and lightness into your life? Is there a habit of seriousness in your life that you need to let go of? Are you in danger of taking yourself too seriously? What physical movement or dance will you do to lighten up? When you find something that works for you and is pleasurable, keep it up. And enjoy!

Chapter 8

Becoming Still To Learn: Mindfulness

*If we knew how important meditation was for the world,
we would meditate as if our hair was on fire.*
                                                Pema Chodron

Mindfulness is the practice of staying present in the moment. It is also called mindfulness meditation and is a type of focused attention. It is a way of being, as opposed to a means to an end. It promotes the understanding that we are already whole. It can be done sitting still, or simply by bringing attention to what is happening right now, whether that is cooking or walking. It offers a comfort zone of stability in the midst of change and chaos. What is most helpful is to cultivate a daily practice, as opposed to doing it once a week or going to a mindfulness retreat once a year. Even five or ten minutes a day will have a huge payoff in terms of increasing self-awareness, calming the nervous system and bringing peace. It softens the ego's sense of being separate and gives us a sense of connection and wholeness.

Through the daily practice of sitting meditation or mindfulness, we can begin to treat ourselves with more softness. Many religious or cultural messages tell us that to love oneself is selfish and wrong and that we should put others first. In fact, until we love ourselves we are shutting off part of our hearts. The message we give to ourselves is: "I'm not worth loving. I don't deserve." Quantum physics teaches us that our thoughts create our reality. If we do not love ourselves, how can we truly love others? As we begin to accept ourselves as we are and open to really loving ourselves unconditionally, our world expands. We start inviting in what we are giving out: unconditional acceptance and love. In accepting ourselves, we automatically become less judgemental of others. What we are striving for is tenderness. We all have a soft spot for someone: our father, our child, our cat perhaps. It helps to sit quietly and bring into our heart that tenderness towards, for example, our cat. From there we can begin to open our hearts to ourselves and let ourselves in, instead of constantly judging ourselves and finding ourselves wanting. The gentler we are with ourselves, the gentler we are with others. So loving Tiddles can begin to engender peace in ourselves and widen to bring more peace into the world. It is a practice. It is a process. It never ends. And that is okay.

Mindfulness is about experiencing the world through the senses; what am I seeing, hearing, touching, smelling and tasting right now? That is why enlightenment is called waking up. Directly sensing the world puts you back in control of your world because you can make new choices and bring your intentions and actions into alignment. Headless chicken living calls you to compare yourself to others and compete with them. The ego always tries to persuade us that in order for us to win, they have to lose. It keeps us stuck in duality. Mindfulness allows you to create mental space, and in that space, you can observe your thoughts. They arise and then they fade away. When they fade away you are still there. This experience teaches us that we are not our thoughts. We are more than our thoughts. The same happens with feelings. They come, they go, and we are still here. They can feel very strong, almost overwhelming, but if we practice mindfulness, we take ourselves back from the edge. We regain control, and there is a proven correlation between feeling in control and low stress levels. Mindfulness allows us to access our treasure trove of inner resources that we are usually cut off from by mindless living. The practice encourages acceptance which is different from resignation. Resignation is passive, apathetic and admits defeat. Acceptance is surrendering to the moment, freeing up a huge amount of energy for life. Resilience improves, as does inner strength, happiness, and joyfulness.

"Doing" mind or ego mind is not an enemy and indeed we couldn't live without it, but it is only suitable for some jobs and not for all tasks of life. There's a saying in Ireland about alcohol or "Drink" as it is better known! "It makes a good servant and a poor master." The same could be said of the ego. When the ego is in charge, we are filled with fears and insecurities and life is a nightmare. When the ego is servant to the Higher Self life is good.

The Gifts of Mindfulness

Teach every eight year old to meditate and we will have eliminated world conflict in one generation.
His Holiness the 14th Dalai Lama

More Self-Awareness

The practice of mindfulness makes us more aware of our thoughts and emotions. It helps us to get to know ourselves better. The practice of mindfulness cultivates the reining in of wayward thoughts that hijack our peacefulness. It helps us redirect our attention towards thoughts that are kind to ourselves. Weakening the ego frees up energy for intensified perception of the beauty of nature and life. It also improves self-discipline, in the following way: we find that our thoughts have wandered and then bring them back to the desired focus of attention. By doing this practice, we lay down the neural pathway for the habit of being able to focus on what we want to focus on. The mind then unconsciously extrapolates from this practice: oh, if I can do this during mindfulness I can also do it while I am working or practising my music/art.

Mindfulness has taught me that I am neither as good as I would like to believe nor as bad as I feared! Phew! I'm average. I'm human. Pretty much the same as most people. And that's a great connector. So mindfulness connects rather than isolates us. As we come to accept our own shadow selves, we are better equipped to accept others as well. Getting to know ourselves better is also helped by reflection from trusted others, so that we can learn who and how we are in the world.

In the stillness of sitting for meditation, awareness can arise. It has the chance to be heard and felt which it doesn't usually have in the rush of our everyday lives. At one time I went through a five year period of stress, loss and grieving. One morning when I was meditating I realised I had become isolated during those years. I had let go of friendships because I was too busy trying to survive. I became aware that during times of stress, one of my patterns is to retreat into my cave. But we are a social species and now the isolation was beginning to hurt. I resolved to start reaching out to people: to reconnect with old friends and meet new ones too. Once an unhealthy pattern emerges into awareness, we have the power to change it for the better. I didn't always find it easy to reach out to people, but I made a start.

One of the tools that supported me in those years of stress was journaling which can put a structure on a wayward internal world. In the new study field of physical intelligence, one experiment divided students into two groups, and asked them to write about a decision that they regretted.[4] One group handed over the piece of paper they had written on while the second group placed it in an envelope before handing it over. They were then asked to rate how negative they felt about the event. Those who had placed the paper in an envelope felt less negative. It was thought that the reason for this was the metaphorical sealing up of the event in the envelope. This ritual can help us release past negative events - by writing them down, sealing them in an envelope – and then burning it safely to release them. It unburdens the soul when we take our thoughts out of our heads and share them, even if it is just with a clean page. It takes the power out of the murky depths and makes the dark thoughts and bad days more manageable. So there is always someone there for us, even if it is just ourselves. We can be our own most powerful and loyal supporter and ally.

Overcoming Opposition

We must continue to open in the face of tremendous opposition. No-one is encouraging us to open and still we must peel away the layers of the heart.
Chogyam Trungpa Rinpoche

Quite often the main source of opposition is our own subconscious mind. It is not surprising when you think about it. We spend years being conditioned by family, society and culture to be a certain way. We are told it is good to be compliant, to keep the rules, to be quiet, to bite back the unbidden retort that comes directly from the heart. We are rewarded for being meek or subservient or appearing calm. We are rewarded for not rocking the boat. This gives the message to our subconscious minds that one part of us is acceptable while other parts are not. We may then unconsciously block ourselves through the mistaken belief that we "don't deserve" good things. Any such belief creates our reality. Even if we find evidence to the contrary of the belief, it will be discounted by our perceptual filter! But those unwanted parts don't go away. They just go underground and emerge eventually, getting our attention through behaviour or habits that cause problems. The practice of sitting still mindfully begins the work of reclaiming those lost parts of ourselves that wanted to shout "Yes" to life, but never got the chance.

One girl I knew said that she had tried mindfulness but gave it up because she couldn't do it as her thoughts kept skittering away. I explained that this is why it is called a practice; it is like trying to keep a toddler sitting on a picnic rug when he wants to be off exploring. You pick him up and put him back down on the rug. In the same way, when our thoughts inevitably wander, once we become aware of the wandering, we just pick them up, label them "Thinking, Thinking," and start again. Or as another piece of sage advice goes – If you are in the kitchen on your own cooking the dinner and the roast falls to the floor, pick it up - because no-one will know!

Compassion

Compassion is that which makes the heart of the good move at the pain of others. It crushes and destroys the pain of others; thus, it is called compassion. It is called compassion because it shelters and embraces the distressed.
Buddha

Compassion expresses the intention of moving from judgement to caring, and from isolation to connection. It is a skill that can be expanded and enhanced with training and practice. Compassion leads to an increase in the DHEA hormone which fights and counteracts the aging process while reducing cortisol, the stress hormone.

The path of compassion does not obligate you to love everyone regardless of how they act or who they are. It is a path of seeing the truth of who they are, acknowledging all their parts...and asking is there anything you can do to heal, assist or bring them in touch with their own higher vision. If there is not, then you are pulling down your own energy by spending time with them.
Sanaya Roman

I have often planted seeds or flowers that took years to bear fruit. I found a rose named Compassion. When I planted it I thought I needed more compassion for others. Now I understand that I needed more compassion for myself and my own struggles. Self-love needs to come first and it then engenders more real love for others. We cannot be more to others than we are to ourselves without a huge cost to our hearts. When we have compassion for ourselves, the identity shift is from the ego to the witness. And as that observer or witness, we can just allow ourselves to be as we are, which is a great relief and a letting go of the strain of trying to be what we are not.

Because we see our thoughts and emotions with compassion, we stop struggling against ourselves.
Pema Chodron

Mindfulness generates compassion. As we stop struggling against ourselves we start being able to allow new energy to flow through us and manifest in our lives. Mindfulness, as an "open ended inquiry into our experience,"[5] (Chodron) leads us to be more open generally. We move away from black or white thinking to direct experience of how things are in the here and now, letting go of wanting them to be a certain way.

The Rapunzel tale tells of a princess locked in a tower who lets her long hair down so that Prince Charming can climb up and free her. The reality is that we have to let our hair down to save ourselves. No-one else is going to save us because no-one else can. Meditation is the key to the locked tower, and once unlocked, we begin to wake up. That is what enlightenment is, waking up to love ourselves and appreciate the amazing world around us. Meditation allows us to use more of our brain power by getting us out of our own way, gently dismantling our inner limits and defences and allowing life to flow through us, unimpeded, without resistance.

Presence versus Absence

*Talk when you talk. Walk when you walk.
Die when you die.*
                                    Zen Proverb

Multitasking is the enemy of presence. I used to be a great multi-tasker. When I started to become mindful, I learned that it was better to just focus on one thing at a time. It allowed me to be more present in my own life and not try to do ten things at one time. So now when I'm eating dinner, instead of reading when I'm alone, I just eat dinner. I look at the plate. After all, I've cooked it. I eat a mouthful and notice what it tastes like. If I read while eating, I look down after a while and the food is gone but I don't remember eating it. I want to lie on my deathbed and remember the important bits of my life. Starting with dinner is as good a place as any. I am not always mindful, but I'm more aware of trying to be mindful now. I practice. It's a start.

Sometimes I really focus, and the rewards are great. I really look and really see. It used to be that those vivid moments of connection with the present moment were rare; thanks to my daily practice of mindfulness, they are becoming more frequent. This morning I breathed in, breathed out as I walked. I looked at the sea and the clouds and the distant hills. I heard the crow cawing on the telephone pole. I heard the waves lapping against the rocks, the sound of the dog's claws on the cement path. I looked and listened as if I would go blind and deaf tomorrow. I was there. This is what my practice is teaching me: to finally descend into my body after years of being absent. To be more fully present in my own life. Mindfulness also yields the gift of our compassionate, attentive presence to others.

Emotions and Mindfulness

Emotion is a process that alerts us to important cues and prepares us to act on them. It includes the perception that something is important, then a body response, an interpretation of the meaning of the cue and then an action. Anger, for example, is a signal that our boundaries have been transgressed. In the body, it is usually experienced in the abdomen and/or back of the neck. On feeling threatened, we get a shot of adrenaline to fuel our fight, flight or freeze mechanism. It stimulates us to take action.

Balanced emotions are neither chaotic nor rigid. The human system is designed to work best in a state of homeostasis or balance. Therefore strong unwelcome emotions are best released to allow health. No strong emotion goes away until it is acknowledged, processed and given space to breathe. Strong emotions also have a message for us; it is important to take the time to listen to what they are telling us, and to take appropriate action. They can be repressed, but it is like trying to keep a balloon under water – it pops back up. Repression uses up a huge amount of life force. It is like having to drag around a huge sack containing all those Things You Don't Want to Face.

If we try to suppress strong emotions by blocking or denying them, they get stuck first in our energy fields, then in our bodies and eventually cause us physical ailments, like low vitality, chronic headaches, or back pains.

Feelings are the language of the soul. In the quiet awareness of mindfulness, any strong, difficult emotion such as anger may arise. When we allow ourselves permission to feel what we feel, without judging ourselves, strong feelings may erupt and pour out of us like a torrent. As we give them permission to be and to flow, emotions eventually subside like flood waters after the storm. They are free to go. In allowing the emotion to be as it is, we are also giving ourselves permission to be as we are, in this moment. There is spaciousness and freedom in that. Letting go of strong emotions gives our souls room to breathe.

Many difficult emotions can be processed through mindfulness, by talking with a wise trusted friend, or through dance or art. But as always, if there has been trauma, or if you are doubtful that you can handle the strong emotion by yourself, err on the side of caution and work with a trusted therapist for containment to avoid being overwhelmed by traumatic memories.

About the Body Scan

*It is much more important to keep
your mindfulness with you than your mobile phone.*
Thich Nhat Hanh

Focusing on our own breath teaches us something very fundamental that many of us have lost: to focus inwards, on ourselves, and begin finding out what is true for us. Beginning to find that we can trust our own body to tell us how we are, our own experience, wisdom and intuition to guide us is a giant step towards reclaiming our power. Instead of constantly looking for answers in the external world, we look to ourselves. The excitement of the next book, teacher, guru or workshop is gradually replaced by the awareness that we can be our own best teacher. Just us and our own breath of awareness.

The practice of the body scan in mindfulness allows us to descend into our bodies. We become absent from our bodies when we live too much in our heads, ruminating over the past or projecting into the future. Being past-focused keeps us mired in stuckness and depression. Living in the future creates anxiety. Future living is the realm of the ego because it is usually fear-based. The ego is thrilled when we are catastrophising in the future. Another reason for being out of our bodies is early trauma, as mentioned before. So it can take a long time to convince our spirit to return to the body. To become whole again. It is like trying to tame a feral cat. You start leaving food out at the end of the garden. The food disappears, so you know the cat is there but you never see it. With patience, gentleness and kindness, you may coax the animal into trusting you and coming inside. It takes as long as it takes to reunite us with ourselves.

The practice of mindfulness, especially the body scan, is a major help. This deceptively simple practice begins to give the message to our subconscious minds that our bodies are fine as they are. They are acceptable exactly as they are. The subconscious mind extrapolates from this and begins to understand that if this is true, then all parts of us are acceptable exactly as they are. It is the antithesis of what we are conditioned to believe. As we do this daily practice, various repressed emotions may arise such as grief, loss, or anger. Whatever arises, just sit with the feelings and let the tears flow and notice that the feelings come, and then they go. Like waves breaking on the shore. Life comes and then goes. This is what the daily mindfulness practice teaches us. Life comes and then goes. In that learning, we begin to value ourselves and our lives more highly. We begin to be more present in our lives instead of thundering through in a rush of commuting and deadlines and duties. In lucid dreaming, we are aware that we are dreaming. As we practice mindfulness, we become aware that we are living. We have more lucid moments where we actually notice where we are and what is happening. Thus, the armoured, icy layers of the heart begin to melt in the sunlight of gentle awareness.

When we begin to be present, anything and anyone can be our teacher. Our minds naturally say, "Oh, this is like that." Life teaches us through everyday things. This is the fruit of the practice of the body scan, where we accept what we find within our physical bodies and let go of the need to have things a certain way. When we start doing that with the body, it spreads out like the ripples from a stone in a lake, affecting our whole lives.

When you rest your awareness in the heart, it is profoundly healing. The heart space opens up, like a deer emerging into a forest clearing. The heart and whole inner self become spacious. And into that space comes peace – "Peace comes dropping slow,"[6] as Yeats said. What also arises is the possibility of a new way of being in the world.

Exercise: The Body Scan

Switch off the phone and make yourself comfortable. Take a deep breath in and as you breathe out, allow your eyes to close. Focus your attention on your breathing. As you breathe in, imagine you are breathing in deep relaxation. As you breathe out, you are beginning to let go. Allow yourself to become quiet inside.

Focus gentle attention on the feet and toes and ask, what is happening here? What do I sense? Notice what is present. Then release them into loving awareness with thanks. Focus on your lower legs. Notice what is present. Release them into loving awareness with thanks. Your thoughts may wander, and if they do, when you become aware of it, just say "Thinking, Thinking," and come back to the body.

Focus on your knees. Notice what is present. Release them into loving awareness with thanks. Focus on your thighs. Notice what is present. Release them into loving awareness with thanks. Focus on your pelvis and all the organs within it. Notice what is present. Release the area into loving awareness with thanks. If your thoughts wander into the future or past, when you become aware of it, just say "Planning, Planning," or "Remembering, Remembering," and then gently come back to the body.

Focus on your lower, middle and upper back. Notice what is present. Release it into loving awareness with thanks. Focus on your abdomen. Notice what is present. Release it into loving awareness with thanks. Focus on your heart. Notice what is present. Release it into loving awareness with thanks. Focus on your arms and hands. Notice what is present. Release them into loving awareness with thanks. Focus on your shoulders, neck and throat. Notice what is present. Release the area into loving awareness with thanks. Focus on your jaw, lips, nose, cheeks, eyes, forehead, scalp and ears. Notice what is present. Release the area into loving awareness with thanks. When you open your eyes, you easily return to full normal awareness feeling calm and relaxed.

Chapter 9

Getting Through Grief and Loss

*It is only with the heart that one can see rightly;
what is essential is invisible to the eye.*
Antoine de Saint Exupéry

We need other humans or animals as expressions of divine love to allow us to experience our own divinity. Grief and loss are inescapable. We can experience loss in so many ways: the loss of a body part, a dream, a precious pet, a beloved person through emigration or death. Grief and loss hollow us out. "Challenges are the fuel for spiritual growth,"[7] as Sonia Choquette says. It is hard to think of heartbreak as a route to spiritual growth when we are going through it. In Tibetan Buddhism, compassion is the capacity to help any living creature at any time. If we allow it, then we can use the pain of grieving to let in more light, more compassion for our own suffering and that of others.

If we are not ready to experience our grief, we need not worry: it will remain on hold for us to deal with when we are ready. It will be there for us when we are strong enough to deal with it.

When we are heartbroken, time has no meaning and grieving can go on for a long time. At this time, the practice of being kind and gentle with ourselves is very important. It is vital that we have compassion for ourselves and our own struggles. To look down the road at years ahead without the beloved is too painful, too overwhelming. It is better to focus just on today, to ask our friends, angels, guides, ancestors, power animals, God and any other potential helpers to assist us in simply getting through this day.

Grief and loss are merciful because they come in

waves. After the tsunami threatens to obliterate us, the tide recedes. The tears come in floods, they recede, and then we wash the dishes. It's like trying to get the house straightened while the baby is asleep. We do what we can when we can. The tears and the washing up all have to be done sometime. We can run, but we can't hide.

In the early days of grief this is our job: to get out of bed when we don't want to, to wash and dress and eat even though we don't feel like it or indeed feel anything at all. We have to stagger through the day's work like the walking wounded that we are.

When the heart is broken, the soul throws out its net to catch the pieces before they drift away forever. That's because the nature of the soul is wholeness. It uses small gestures and simple pleasures to begin to bind the broken shards back together. It uses the soft words of a friend, your dog's paw on your knee, the sound of your cat purring. It uses the warmth of the first spring sun on your face after a long cold winter.

With every day that goes by, our souls are at work, slowly supergluing the broken bits back together. Our job is to just hold on. And get through it we do, even though it feels like we never will. Quite often the main source of pressure on us to progress or "move forward" is ourselves. It is kinder to hear those harsh inner voices and just ignore them, and instead allow ourselves to just get through another day as we heal. Moving on will come in its own time.

The Experience of Loss

Love will always know its own, for love is the greatest force in the universe. Love will always attract its beloved and love will always meet its love, for nothing can prevent the union of those who love.
Silver Birch (When asked how we can find our loved ones in spirit after we die.)

It might bring great comfort at a funeral if instead of saying, "Remember man thou art but dust," the minister said: "Remember man thou art but love and into love thou shall return." It would be more accurate, too.

After a time, grief subsides. When it subsides, loss is left. However impossible it seems while we are going through the anguish, we can come to a place of acceptance. As weeks turn to months and years, it is as if the sharp edges of our grief are rounded down to become more bearable. We may get to the place where we would not wish to have the person back if they were suffering before they died. Or maybe we can find some sort of reason why they are gone, something that is meaningful and valid to us. But the space where the person – or animal - used to be is with us forever. Loss can resonate for many years, catching us unawares.

After my father died, I experienced loss like an underground river that would erupt from a hidden place at the strangest of times. Out cycling in the sun in the back lanes of the Majorcan countryside, tears spilled from my eyes when I saw the beauty of the place and hoped that my Dad's place in the spirit sun was as beautiful. Months later, after a relatively calm period of acceptance, over breakfast one morning I suddenly realised I hadn't seen him in four years and a wave of loss washed over me. "I miss you," my heart cried.

As Silver Birch says, "Those you love and who love you are never lost to you…sometimes you are sad and shed tears and wash your loved ones away."

In moments of calm stillness, when we are not submerged in grief, we may sense them close to us. This is real. We are bound to our beloved ones by a matrix of love, energy, attention and devotion. This matrix is woven into the fabric of our cells. That is why, if we can allow the understanding in, our beloved is not lost to us through physical death. They are literally part of us, always with us. As Lynne McTaggart says in The Field: "Things once in contact remain in contact through all space and time."[8]

The theory of quantum entanglement essentially says that once we have shaken hands with someone, our atoms are forever connected. Once we have loved someone, the love remains even when the body is no longer present.

Gentler Questions

Grieving is the process of trying to come to terms with the shock and trauma of separation from our beloved. Love is so central to us that to lose a beloved is akin to our own death. In the days, weeks, months and years after a huge loss, we are unconsciously trying to give birth to our new self, the self we are without the loved one. We are unconsciously striving for the wholeness that we felt with our beloved. We are unconsciously trying to integrate the parts of ourselves that have been wandering in the wastelands of pain. In this context, we have to ask the right question to help ourselves, because to ask the wrong question is like pouring bleach onto an open wound. The wrong question such as "Why did this happen?" is not just useless, not just crazymaking, but actively heaps anguish onto suffering. We cannot know why things happen until we are back in spirit and able to access the bigger picture.

A gentler, kinder, more useful question is: "How will I get through this day?" (Or this hour, when things are really bad.) Another gentle question is "What painful thoughts can I let go of now to make space for comfort to come into my heart?"

As my grieving for my father changed shape, I learned this: If we are lucky enough to have a precious moment to hold on to, we can choose to focus on that, as opposed to the painful ones. I chose to remember one early winter day. I had helped my Dad with his walker onto the concrete in the back yard. He sat in the wintry sun, wrapped up against the chill. One of the cats basked in the sun beside us. He dozed for a while then woke suddenly, looked around at the sun, the cat and me and said "Peace." Then he promptly fell asleep again.

If we have such a nugget of comfort, let us be keenly aware of it. That way, we can gently pull it out of our pocket to feast on when we need the sustenance most, like a life-giving glucose sweet when we are in danger of dying of hunger.

Sometimes how others cope with loss or trauma can inspire us. A woman I know came home from work and found her husband hanging in the shed. This had happened three years prior to my meeting her. This woman had the most positive life force and attitude to life I've ever seen. "How did you get through it so well?" I asked her. "I found one good thing to focus on each day," she said. Whether it was a flower in bloom or her pet dog, that's what she focused on with gratitude. She narrowed her focus of attention to that one good thing each day, which in turn gave her heart and spirit time to heal.

I met an artist who was doing a retrospective of the last four years of her work. "That's how long it took me to process my father's death," she said. At the time, I foolishly thought that was a bit excessive. Now I know differently. Four years after the loss of my own father, I understand what she meant.

Society gives the message that we may be allowed grieve for a few months after the death of a loved one. But the heart doesn't care about clocks. As Blaise Pascal said, "The heart has reasons that reason knows not of."[9] It can be a lonely journey. There are few people in whom we can confide the depth of our ongoing grief and loss. We are expected to just "get on with it." It helps the process if the grieving person feels they can speak openly of the difficulties involved; how they may have become isolated, not having had the emotional energy to answer letters, texts or phone calls. How they put their head down on the table and cried when trying to figure out how the boiler works, because that was always their partner's job. How they don't have the energy to do the things they used to love, that nourished and supported them; how they fear going back to work or their club activities, because of a dread of being unable to cope. How they saw a neighbour while out shopping and went home to tell their spouse, forgetting he was gone. How they saw a blue scarf the colour of their child's eyes, which set them off crying in the middle of the department store. We need to listen to their pain and give them the space to breathe or cry or be angry or lonely. Because there is nothing surer - our turn will come.

    I spent a lot of time holding my father's hand in the months leading up to his death. I was lucky to have the chance to do so. I became familiar with its weight, the calluses from years of hard work, its' shape. The dark hair on the back of his hand and fingers. The warmth of it as the blood still fed his body. The hand of hands that had worked so hard. That had held mine as a child, warm and comforting. At his funeral, as I looked into the hole in the ground that held his coffin, a roar of grief erupted from me as I realised I would no longer have his body, his person to look after. His absence would be my companion for life. I miss holding his hand. I miss everything about him, and it's been years. In my heart, I will always miss him. I miss his presence. His absence is with me always even though I know in my heart we are still connected by love.

    Looking back now, however, I understand this: I didn't need to give the pain as much time as I did. We can recover from the loss of a beloved; we can come to an accommodation of their absence as a constant presence. On my next cycle of grieving, I hope to recover faster, because now I have integrated what I learned from the most recent loss. It is okay to recover our wholeness and feel better. And the sooner the better. It is what our loved ones in spirit want for us because they are feeling great where they are. They are wrapped in the cocoon of unconditional love from which they came, from which we all came. They are okay now. They are safe and well.

Visualisation: Lovingkindness Meditation

Switch off the phone and make yourself comfortable. Take some deep breaths to centre yourself. With each breath you take, allow yourself to become more and more relaxed. Soften the eyes, chest, and belly. Let the shoulders drop. Bring your attention to your heart. Place the first two fingers of your right hand on your heart. Breathe in and out, as if the heart and the breath were one. Let your right hand drop gently now onto your knee. Now imagine yourself as a young child. Bring that image or sense or knowingness into your heart. Imagine pink and green light surrounding this child and all the gifts it brought into this world to share. Keep your body and breath soft and gentle. Now imagine or sense your heart expanding as you bring a beloved person or animal into your heart. Surround them with green and pink light and love. Feel your heart soften even more. Expand your heart beyond the room, the city, the country until it encompasses the whole world. Let that loving pink and green light go to every sentient being, every animal and insect and bird, every plant and tree and flower. Let it go to the earth itself, and the ocean, and the sky. Let the entire world and everything in it be bathed in the gentle light of lovingkindness and know yourself to be connected, supported, worthy and loved simply because you exist.

Chapter 10

Resurrecting Dreams and Living Your Life Purposefully

Twenty years from now, you will be more disappointed by the things you didn't do, than by the things you did. So throw off the bowlines, sail away from the safe harbour. Catch the trade winds in your sails.
Explore. Dream. Discover.

Mark Twain

Soul Purpose

When you are young, you think you will live forever. You think that you will always have the time and opportunities to do whatever you want to do. Then life or work gets in the way, and suddenly, the landscape has changed. So many women panic in their mid-thirties, as they discover they have career success but no children. Even if you think you don't want children, the impact of the biological imperative to reproduce has to be experienced to be believed. It's like the menopause – you wouldn't believe that the dropping of three itty bitty hormone levels could cause such chaos in your life.

So whether it is travel or a study course you always wanted to do, begin now. The things our souls want us to do may have no apparent purpose but I guarantee there IS a purpose. It may be someone we are to meet, who will open our eyes to a new perspective or truth. Or maybe there is someone WE are to help. These soul longings never go away because they are vital. They are woven into our bones. We ourselves decided the things we wanted to experience in this incarnation before we came into this life. That is why they are so important. They are not frivolous. From the higher perspective of being in spirit between lives, in consultation with our guides, we agreed that this is what we wanted. And then we come into these bodies, forget our soul agreements, and spend most of our lives denying or ignoring what we ache for inside.

Quite often, when we are children, we know what we want to do with our lives but the adults tell us no, that wouldn't be possible, or there are no jobs in that area, or no money in it, and we put away our "childish" dreams. But our childish dreams are usually the key to our life purpose.

From an early age, I knew I wanted to be a writer. I loved animals and also wanted to work with them or help them in some way. I remember looking around at my family when I was seven and thinking, this would make a great story. My young self knew I wanted to be a writer. I loved writing English essays and laboured over them with love. But of course, for final school exams, time is of the essence. My teacher had encouraged me but had warned that I wouldn't have time to write such great essays or original analyses of the books on the course in the final exam. He was right. My co-students who memorised the standard answers from exam study notes and regurgitated them did far better than I did. I didn't really care about the rest of the subjects, but I was crushed about my English exam results. The mark I had hoped for and worked hard for did not materialise. I felt I had failed, even though I had passed. That was because I mistakenly equated school exam results with being a writer. It took me over twenty years to recover my confidence and start writing again. When I look back at that wasted time, I shake my head now in disbelief and with a wry smile. I detoured through becoming a general and paediatric nurse and clinical hypnotherapist. And I learned a lot by doing those things.

Yet, here I am now, writing a book, showing up at the page. Better late than never. And I found, once I started practising, words and stories and poems flowed out of me. And at my age, it's okay to be original. No exams now. There is no-one to tell me now that exams are more important than actual literature, writing or life.

When my best friend and soul mate (soulmates are often friends and not always partners, by the way) was eleven, she knew children who finished primary education without being able to spell or do basic maths. She knew she wanted to help them. She detoured through a degree in French and History and selling washing machines before becoming an adult literacy tutor in her forties.

My seventy-six year old friend bemoans that she doesn't have a degree in psychology. She felt she couldn't start it now because she can no longer drive herself to college. What about the Open University, I asked? I never thought of that, she said. Her body may be a bit frail in places but her mind is fine and her heart is huge. She will still be eighty in four years, so I hope she goes for it. It is only ourselves that hold us back from at least attempting our dreams. Even if it doesn't pan out, at least we can give it a try and die having tried, all used up and with no regrets.

Being and Doing

I used to think that a life purpose was something I had to do, some job. As a volunteer in Dog's Aid Animal Sanctuary, I have often sat with two cats on my knee, surrounded by more cats. One day as I was giving them healing while feeling their fur and hearing them purring, I realised I had been wrong. Our life purpose is not about doing, it's about being. Whatever we choose to do is just the framework, the structure to allow us to be our infinite selves. I am most myself when I am surrounded by animals, especially cats. This is me. This is my True Self. My Divine Self. There's nothing more I have to do other than sit with cats and enjoy them. That's enough.

Our egos want to pay the bills and know where the money is coming from; our souls don't care – they just want to dance and be joyful. Or sit with cats and be joyful. Ego living is worry and strife. Soul living is letting go, enjoying what is and getting out of our own way.

I was in my own way most of my life. I always knew that meditation would be a life changer for me, which is why my ego resisted it so hard for so long. My ego was right to be afraid, very afraid! Now when I become aware of the voice of my ego, I imagine my angels or guides leading a tired child off for a nap. Since starting to meditate daily, I have come on in leaps and bounds. I understand now, at a visceral level, what I only understood intellectually before. Sometimes I slip into ego mode and become fearful. When that happens, as soon as I become aware of it, I do something different. I sit with the fear in meditation or do some energy healing on myself. I might have a massage to bring me back into my body in the here and now, or read a book to remind me of what I already know: soul living is easier and more enjoyable. Once I relax and let go, the flow starts again and all is well. I become more hopeful and optimistic and I'm back on track. My aim is to spend more time being happy, contented and joyful and less time being stressed and fearful. And if I manage that eighty percent of the time, that's good enough. I don't have to be perfect. Good enough will do.

Another gift of meditation is to increase self-discipline and self-mastery so that we become more able to allow ourselves to do what we need to do. To sit and write a book, paragraph by paragraph or make a wood cabinet – whatever our souls are calling us to do. It doesn't matter what we do. It matters how we feel about what we do. Sometimes I do an animal healing session, and I see the animal go from being tense, stressed or anxious to relaxing completely and maybe going asleep as the heat in my hands releases the stress from their system. It is such a pleasure and a privilege for me to do the work, that to get paid for it by a private client is the icing on the cake. It gives me a sense of at least doing part of what I came here to do. It fills me up.

Investigating What We Want

Sometimes when we hear of people doing amazing things it inspires us. At other times it may overwhelm us, leading us to think, oh, what's the use, I could never do that. The good news is that not only do we NOT have to do what others do, but indeed, even if we try, it won't work for us.

There's a story about a woman who quietly started making sandwiches for her local homeless shelter. She delivered them on her lunch break. Word got out and her colleagues did a money collection and gave it to her to help her make more sandwiches. She took the money and went away and thought about it. The next day she went into work and left the money in the staffroom. She put a note on the noticeboard: "Thanks but make your own damn sandwiches." The point is that we have to do our OWN investigation to find out what is the right thing for us to do; no-one else can do this task for us.

We have to use our own unique gifts, talents and callings to create our own form of service to the world. I have studied a lot about how to discover your life purpose and this is what I now believe: it is much simpler than you think. Our life purpose is to become aware of our gifts and then use them, whatever they may be.

In a nutshell:

Just find what you love to do. Then do it.

Simple does not necessarily mean easy, but for our souls to expand, we need to do it anyway, hard or easy. Sure, you may have to experiment with many different variations to hit on what works for you. It may take you fifty years or more. Additionally, what works for you now will not be the same in five or ten years' time, because you will not be the same either.

Service

> *Human consciousness can only evolve through individual effort.*
> Sandra Corcoran, Shaman

There is a need to serve. This might sound onerous, but in fact, when we find the thing we came here to do, we can be happy and also serve a greater purpose. Allowing ourselves to be happy raises our vibration and that in itself helps the world. The old idea of this life as a "vale of tears" to be stoically borne until we go into the next life is defunct. In fact, the more we are true to ourselves and commit ourselves to whatever our life purpose is, the more light we bring into the world. We need not worry that we will be too happy because loss, grief and death are all part of life and we will still have to deal with them. However, there is nothing to be gained from wallowing in misery either. Research has shown that those who volunteer altruistically (with the intention of helping others as opposed to making themselves feel better) are likely to feel more socially connected, have lower stress levels and lower blood pressure.

As Jack Kornfield says, "It's not that we have to get into the flow of the river, we ARE the river." It really helps to set your intention and then follow where you are lead. Just do the best you can, where you are, with what you've got, whether it is picking up other peoples' litter or employing ten people. That's all. Your heart will do the rest and your soul will continually strive to wake you up to truth. The truth is that you are an infinite being with infinite possibilities. Our potential to be ourselves and to be great is within each of us, waiting for us to invite it into being. Within the framework of our passions, and our soul's plan for us, we can achieve exactly what we need to be more whole and complete.

Exercise: Discovering What Is Important

Have your journal and a pen to hand.

Switch off the phone and make yourself comfortable. Take a deep breath in and as you breathe out, allow your eyes to close. Focus your attention on your breathing. As you breathe in, imagine you are breathing in deep relaxation. As you breathe out, you are beginning to let go. Soften the eyes, the chest, and the belly. Let the shoulders drop as if you are leaving down your burdens. Imagine there is a Divine light of protection around you now and at all times. Allow yourself to become quiet and still inside. Imagine that you are lying on your deathbed. You look back over your life and smile at the good things and good people you remember, the highlights. You may become sad at some memories, which is to be expected. Now you gently become aware of some regrets about things you did not do or try. There was something that you would LOVE to have tried out or done or become if you had the chance again. Allow yourself to become aware of what it is. It may come to you as a word, a symbol or an awareness. Allow yourself time to explore it. You find it easy to remember when you open your eyes and you write it down straight away.

Now look at what you have written in your journal. What action can you take to begin to allow this into your life in a way that is meaningful and valid for you?

What are your gifts? Make an honest list of them and in doing so acknowledge what you have to offer the world. What do you love doing? What is the worst thing that could happen if you tried something and it didn't work out? At least, you would have the pride in yourself that you gave it a try. Of course, to complete a goal, we have to get back up, dust ourselves off, and go for Plan B. And keep going until Plan Z, if necessary, until we are done. It may bring you down a different road to the one you originally imagined. That's okay. It's part of the fun. "Resistance is futile," as The Borg used to say on Star Trek, The Next Generation. I changed it to "Resistance is futile, but perseverance is vital." A world of adventure opens up to us when we leave the safe harbour of what we have always done, and embark on a thrilling voyage towards our dreams – whatever they may be. Honour them. Godspeed.

Chapter 11

Becoming Authentic

If you're not always wanting, you can be at peace.
And if you're not always trying to be someone
You can be who you really are
And go the whole way.

Tao Te Ching

Who Am I?

Many of us have lost contact with our real selves. We lost that contact by constantly denying our own needs. Of course, if you are a mother with children or a carer looking after an elderly parent, their needs come first. But somehow, somewhere along the line, it is necessary to carve out a space for ourselves, no matter what the situation. The cost of not doing this is too high. The cost is our authentic selves. When we are split from our real selves, we have lost access to our energy core. When the child grows up and leaves or the parent dies, we find we are empty and lost. We have no Northern Star to guide us because we were so subsumed in the role of parent or carer we don't know who we are without that job. We have over-identified with that role.

Make no mistake, the search for identity is the search for our soul. We are like snakes needing to shed their skins to get a new one. It is as if, when the understanding dawns on us that we really, really are getting older and we really, really are going to die, then putting up with nonsense is such a waste of time. Periodically, as we grow, we outgrow some people, pursuits and places. We need new friends who only know us as we now are, as well as old friends who have known us forever. We humans have a need to know ourselves through the reflection of others; that is why it is important to be discerning about with whom we spend our time. It is no judgement on another if we let that friendship go. It is simply that we are different now, our energy is different, and we need different things. To paraphrase Oscar Wilde, the only certainties in life are death, taxes – and change. Without change, there is stasis and a withering of our life force.

Speaking Out From the Heart

> *If there is something to say, one must not be silent.*
> *To be silent is to die.*
> Andalusian Goat Herder
> and Siguiya Flamenco Dancer

It can take us a long time to speak out. The inner self knows what the truth is. This is the self that will start asking inconvenient questions like, "Is this it? Is this as good as it gets?" These questions are uncomfortable but necessary because life is short. The older we get, the more we really understand this as we see friends and family members die. A panic can set in and that is no bad thing. Anything that serves to wake us up to who we really are and what we really want is good. We don't have to wait until we are terminally ill to realise that life is precious. I believe in reincarnation, but live as if this is the only life I have. It may well be. I'm not taking any chances anymore!

Failing to speak our truth costs us at a soul level because the soul thrives on truth. A tart response springs to our lips but we suppress it to "keep the peace." Whose peace? What peace? Not our own peace of mind, that's for sure. We don't want to upset the applecart. If the issue is trivial, this is not a problem. If it goes against our values or means our rights are being contravened, big problem. "Explode or corrode" is a therapy term used to describe this state. And corrode we do. We become constantly tired, listless, lacking life energy for our daily lives. We may develop an illness, minor or major. The body never lies. It tells the truth of what is happening if we will only listen.

One woman I know had four children. Her husband was a bully. She told him she was leaving him. It took her four years to gather the resources to do it. But do it she did. She was afraid of him, but she did it anyway. If she had waited *until* she felt powerful, she would still be living with him, with him bullying her and the children. It's okay to be afraid. It's not okay to be emotionally abused, or physically abused, or bullied. It's not okay to allow it to happen to children. That woman now has peace of mind and the knowledge of her own courage. She gave her children a powerful life lesson too, in taking action to end oppression. She has regained her own power because she was true to herself.

The Blues

When I sing the blues, it comes from the heart. From right here in your soul, an' if you're singing what you feel it comes out all over. It ain't just what you sayin', it pours out of you. Sweat running down your face.

Muddy Waters

When we express ourselves from the heart, we are tapping into a huge reservoir of spiritual energy. We need to let our unique energy out there into the external world, whether it's by singing or writing or baking cakes. Strong feelings need expression or they go underground and cause us problems. So get your ukulele, pen or mixing bowl out and let your heart speak its truth. Life gets better when you do.

Make no mistake, changing our lives for the better is anything but comfortable. Change is not easy. It takes courage. Our habits and routines make us feel safe. Some people say to me, "Things can only get better." I disagree. That argument is a justification for staying stuck. Things can either stay the same or get worse. Einstein said the definition of madness was doing the same thing over and over and expecting a different result. Unless we change and DO something different, one day we will just look in the mirror and see an old person who says, "It's too late for me to change now." To make our lives better, we need to initiate change, fear or no fear.

We may know that deep down, our job does not fulfil us, but our logical mind thinks, well, I have another hundred years on the mortgage, so I'll just have to stick it out. Sometimes our jobs can be a "honey trap." The job provides security and perhaps has implications for pension payments in the future. That is okay if we are finding a way to honour our soul's purpose. If we are not, then the job and its apparent security are a trap. Because there may not be a future. Would you stay in your current job if you knew you only had one year to live?

Of course, we have to find a way to pay the bills. We have to be practical dreamers with the courage to jump in. One man I know worked in a boring government job that guaranteed security. He hated it but needed the money. He balanced it by carving wood, being in a choir and going skydiving. By honouring his desire for adventure, he honoured his soul. After a few years, the "real self" that emerged through these apparent "pleasurable hobbies" became too restless to contain. He went back to college to retrain in a completely different field. He then left the government job. He earns less now but the bills are still paid and he is content. That contentment is priceless. Note that the process took a few years. Best to get started now!

So get the show on the road. Allow yourself to become aware of whatever you need to do. Let it incubate in the fertile back burner of your deep mind if you don't have the immediate wherewithal to do it. Ask your ancestors for prayers or help. Ask your angels and spirit guides for help. Ask human friends for support and good thoughts. When help arrives, and it will, accept it and say thank you. (Your turn will come to help others.) Daily mindfulness practice will keep you centred in the storm of emotion (yours and others') that arises when you no longer want to cooperate with being unhappy.

Remember: there will never be a perfect time. Waiting until your ducks are all in a row is just another excuse. The right time is when you are as ready as you can be. I went to learn how to paraglide when I was fifty. Standing on the edge of a mountain, strapped to the instructor for my first tandem flight, she asked was I ready. Was I ready to jump off a high mountain attached to a bit of fabric? No. I wasn't. "Er...no," I squeaked. "But let's go anyway." As one of my cats, Tilly, says: "Feel the fur and do it anyway!"

When you finally meet yourself, "arrive at your own door," as Jon Kabat-Zinn says, it can be an emotional experience. Tears may flow. That's okay. It is just the frozen tundra of your heart thawing, opening to yourself, allowing integration with the true self to take place. It is a powerful moment. It is an empowering step on your spiritual journey. Things will never be the same again because you cannot unknow your essence, your true self. You then have to find a new way to be in the world. And more than that, meeting your True Self is no less than meeting the Divine. It is simple, unadorned and potent power to come face-to-face with yourself and realise who you truly are. There is no going back after that.

Integrity

To thine own self be true.
William Shakespeare

The word integrity means wholeness, uprightness, honesty, purity. It is important for us to move towards integrity, and in so doing, bring more of that wholeness into the world. How do we become whole? We listen to the quiet but insistent urgings of our souls and take action on that guidance.

Acknowledging the Shadow Self

> *Knowing your own darkness is the best method for dealing with the darkness's of others.*
> Carl Jung

The shadow self is the darker part of each of us that we fail to own. In order to mine the gold in the shadow self, we need to acknowledge our potential to think and act negatively. These destructive tendencies are reactions of the ego. A healthy ego is necessary to negotiate daily life, but it makes a better passenger than driver. By failing to accept these negative tendencies, we give them power. What we react strongly to in others usually points to something within ourselves that we are denying. In this way, we project our negative aspects onto others. When we begin the process of accepting that we have the capacity to be unkind, cruel or destructive, the ego loses more power and the Higher Self can step in. After all, what is so bad about having these tendencies – unless we act on them? By accepting our dark side, we gain a huge amount of power and energy to fuel our creativity and the move to wholeness. Moment by moment, day by day we are faced with the choice to think, say or do what will bring us on the higher or lower path; to think, say or do the right or wrong thing according to our internal moral compass. We do not need to get it right all the time. Indeed, mistakes are unavoidable because we are here on Earth to learn, and we learn through mistakes. In Spirit, all is perfect, so that is why the Earth school is so useful. Doing the right thing is unlikely to be easy. And it can be especially hard when we see politicians or public power figures that have caused harm not only "get away with it" but be rewarded for it. It is better to look inside for guidance and bring awareness to how the body reacts to our actions. A feeling of relaxation or expansion indicates a good decision in line with our soul, and a feeling of contraction, tension or stress indicates that a better choice is possible.

Our daily practice of mindfulness or meditation helps us slowly, slowly, to become more whole. Our reward is that we are granted access to more of who we really are. Our true selves. We gradually become less Headless Chicken and more Zen Hen. We calm down. The ego, of course, resists. It does everything it can to throw obstacles in the way of our practice. "I'm tired," it whines: "I won't bother doing it today. Tomorrow will do. There's a film on TV I want to see. There's a friend I want to meet." And so on. More than anything, the ego is threatened by wholeness. Just listen, nod – and do the practice anyway.

What emerges from the practice is the space to be ourselves. "To thine own self be true" – now that you are beginning to know who to be true to. And it will emerge in your daily life. Someone will say something that jars with you and you will notice. That is usually because they have a different set of values to yours. Your job then is to only say what is true for you, only agree to what is right for you, and to let go of old habits of people-pleasing or soothing or comforting. If you don't have the energy to challenge the person, then take Seamus Heaney's advice: "Whatever you say, say nothing." Don't sell your soul for the sake of peace because it doesn't work. You just end up with less of your soul and still the strife remains. Being true to yourself may spark conflict with others because you are no longer dancing to their tune. You are marching to the drum of your own soul instead. Initial discomfort is worth the relaxation in the gut that comes with being true to yourself. It grounds you and makes you more solid, gives you back your power and gives you the energy to begin to change your world for the better.

Freedom

*Freedom is not doing whatever you want to do;
freedom is wanting whatever needs to be done
to grow to our full stature.*
Mark Patrick Hederman,
Abbot of Glenstal Abbey

There is no "one day." There is only today. Now is the moment of pure potential. What does freedom mean to you? Are you waiting for permission to do something with your life? Once you are an adult, you have no excuses left. There will never be a good time. True, there are some times that would be impossible. But there is never a perfect time to switch off the television and pay attention to your dreams. Freedom means taking responsibility. We have no-one to blame anymore. There is only us, today and what we choose to do with it.

Permission

*To be what we are
and to become what we are capable of becoming
is the only end in life.*
Robert Louis Stevenson

We hold ourselves back in so many ways. We are frequently less than we could be. In my work as a past life regression therapist, I always ask a client who is undergoing regression what regrets they have as they look back over the life they are exploring. The most common regret is "I should have loved more." I never once heard anyone saying "I should have made more money."

Love themselves, love others. It's all the same love. Years ago, I took my beloved cat to a healer because she had cancer. "Is it different from the healing you do on people?" I asked. "No," he said. "Healing is healing." It is. I know that now, having become a healer myself. And love is love. We can only love others to the extent that we love ourselves. In giving permission to ourselves to sit and be with ourselves for a *whole ten minutes* of mindfulness practice each day, we are indirectly giving ourselves permission to be as we are. We begin to open the door of understanding to our innermost hearts.

Anita Moorjani, who had a Near Death Experience (NDE), writes: "When we say that people are of a higher vibration, we probably mean that they're letting more of their authentic magnificence come through - consequently their positive energy and physical presence are strong."[10]

So being ourselves is the choice for strength and power. When our life force is strong, our aura becomes more charismatic or "attractive," attracting more of what we want (and will allow) into our lives. It is enlightened self-interest to become our real selves.

Practice and the Ego

The ego wants us to be safe. It wants us to believe we are small and should not take chances. This is a lie. Our true selves are limitless, expansive, eternal, and powerful with the capacity to feel great joy. So when your soul beckons, the ego becomes afraid.

For example, my ego resisted my attempts to meditate regularly for years. Oh, I tried. And I did meditate. But I couldn't do it consistently. It was as if my ego knew how powerful such a simple process could be. How transformative. I once did a constellation therapy day. It's a kind of group therapy energy work based on Bert Hellinger's work. It acknowledges that we may not only be carrying our own suffering but the unresolved suffering of our ancestors. I chose someone to represent me and observed the outcome. What transpired was that I was at odds with myself. I was approaching my True Self but not integrating her. "Years of resistance," said the facilitator. He was right. Years of not being myself. Years of abrogating my needs for the needs of others. I had thought I was doing the right thing. But it turned out that one thing I needed to do was carve out the time and space to be myself. To give myself the chance to listen, feel and act on my OWN behalf. So many of us put our lives on hold for months or years. Then suddenly we are in our sixties or seventies and time is running out. When you are young, you believe you are immortal. And indeed, your soul and spirit are immortal. But your physical body is not. It wears out. The grains of sand in the egg timer run out and that's it, you're dead.

When your soul makes you aware that all your life you have wanted to be a gardener or an artist, you ego will immediately jump in and say, "Don't be ridiculous! You couldn't do that. Just put up and shut up. Forget about it." The voice is persuasive and pervasive. It probably sounds like the bully who sneered at you at school or the teacher who squashed your dreams with a few well-chosen words. The ego is threatened by anything that may be positive, transformative or life changing for the better. It thrives on routine and fear.

But there is a way around it. In order to fly under the radar of its resistance, we have to be devious. One way I have found is to label important work as "practice." Oh, I'm not really writing a book – I'm just practising. The ego subsides, reassured. After all, she's not doing anything important or useful – she's just practising. Oh, I'm not meditating or being assiduous with mindfulness – I'm just practising. The ego subsides.

In the space that is created, there is an opportunity to be creative, to tap into the deeper levels of ourselves and nurture our souls, by writing or sitting looking at our breath, or gardening, or playing with the cat – the myriad simple things that we love doing but rarely give ourselves permission to do. There are so many other apparently important things to do - while our souls languish from lack of nurturing. The small, simple things are full of soul satisfaction. They allow us moments of joy, of contentment in our own skins.

Your Challenge

Take pen and paper. Complete the following sentence:
"If there was something important I would love to say and need to say, but have not yet found the courage, I would say..........." Then imagine the person in front of you and say the words out loud. This is a rehearsal, and it helps to bring the words out into the open and hear yourself saying them. It brings you one step closer to actually saying what needs to be said.

Chapter 12

Gathering Resources for the Journey

In order truly to be generous with one another, we require whatever level of prosperity allows us such generosity.
                                                       Rosalyn Bruyere, Healer

Abundance and Prosperity

Because we live in a physical world, sometimes we need money, help or opportunities in order to manifest the positive changes we want so that we can live our best lives. In learning how to love ourselves, the process of mindfulness helps us realize that we are not disconnected from others. It also helps us to realize we are connected to the Source, however we may perceive that to be. Once we understand that the true nature of life is to have what we need, our job is to then offload the beliefs and conditioning that shaped us to expect scarcity.

In her book "Dying to be Me," Anita Moorjani provides a fascinating insight into abundance consciousness that arose during her near death experience. She writes:

"Since the tapestry of all time has already been woven, everything I could ever want to happen in my life already exists in that infinite, non-physical plane. My only task is to expand my earthly self enough to let it into this realm. So if there's something I desire, the idea isn't to go out and get it, but to expand my own consciousness to allow universal energy to bring it into my reality here."

It has taken me years to really, really understand how manifesting abundance works. In the hope of speeding things up for you so that you can manifest whatever you need when you need it (such as money, time, helpful people, or opportunities,) here is a distilled version of what I have learned.

1. Money is just a form of energy that needs to be used and exchanged. It is not intended to be hoarded, any more than you would attempt to hoard life energy from one day to the next.

2. Whatever we choose to focus on increases. The universe responds in kind, either way, by reflecting back to us our precise belief through the experience we are offered.

3. We are constantly attracting something into our lives; we can choose to do it more consciously and get what we want, or just take pot luck and often receive what we do not want.

4. What we attract depends on our beliefs. Our beliefs act like magnets, for good or bad. How we choose to think about money upholds our beliefs about it. If our thoughts are productive, it flows easily in and out of our life.

5. If our thoughts are on the lack or scarcity of money, it dries up. If we focus on being broke, it brings us more experience of being broke.

Letting Go of Scarcity

Thoughts such as "money doesn't grow on trees" reflect the scarcity mentality which may have arisen from the way we were brought up. For instance, my parents grew up during WW2. My mother often spoke of what was not available – items such as tea, flour, or tyres for bicycles (few people had cars at the time). She sometimes mentioned playing cards or tennis because there was no television. My father occasionally mentioned the scarce things, but also talked about cycling twenty five miles each way to the races in Punchestown with his mother and brother, and the fun they had, even though they had little money. It was the same country, but they each had different perceptions of the situation. Overall, it sounds like there was much less comfort than today but more opportunities for fun, more physical fitness, and more community spirit.

The energy of scarcity is contraction. It is low vibration energy. By contrast, the energy of abundance is high vibration. Scarcity says "No" to so many things, while abundance says "Yes, bring it on NOW!!!" Scarcity implies that not only is there not enough for us but there is certainly not enough to share with anyone else. In this sense, holding on to a scarcity mentality really limits our lives and our spiritual growth. Source/God/The Creator Spirit is abundant, exuberant, ever expanding. When Jesus was faced with five thousand mouths to feed, he didn't just feed the few people near him and say to everyone else, "That's it folks, tough luck." The message was that there is more than enough for everyone. Also, note that an elite few did not take the breadbasket and hold on to the contents, keeping more for themselves and their cronies and depriving the masses of basic food! Instead, everyone got fed. Everyone went home with a full belly. Jesus then directed the apostles to gather up the leftovers which filled twelve baskets. To me, implicit in the gathering up of leftovers is respect for resources. Nothing goes to waste. I like that. Additionally, Jesus did not try preaching to people who had hungry bellies. We have to nurture the body before we can nurture the spirit because at this time we live in a physical universe.

Think of expanding into abundance as a boat journey. A clear intention with strong desire is like deciding to visit a destination and believing it is possible. That is like setting the dial on the GPS of the boat. Preparation for the journey includes clearing out the boat and making sure that only essentials are taken on the voyage. In this case, the preparation is the clearing out of old conditioning and beliefs that limit prosperity. Provisioning the boat for the journey involves making sure that only useful beliefs are going with us. There is no room for mental drivel or negativity. Then, in order to create positive change, we need to untie the mooring rope, switch on the engine and leave the safe harbour for the open sea of possibilities. We need to allow the journey to happen. Keeping a gentle hand on the tiller to make sure we stay on course and then - let it be.

The Sequence of Manifestation

- Desire
- Belief
- Expectancy
- Visualisation
- Action
- Surrender
- Manifestation

1. Desire: Desire is a powerful motivating force. You have to be very clear on what you want, and that you really want whatever it is. Write down the answers to these two questions: What will having this do for me? How will I feel when I have it? Being clear on your intention is essential. A useful tool to focus your desire is to create a vision board. Use colourful images that represent your goal AS IF IT HAD ALREADY MANIFESTED. The language of the subconscious mind, the

powerhouse of all change, involves colour, shapes, imagery and symbolism. Place your vision board in a prominent place and frequently focus your attention on it.

2. Belief: W. Clement Stone said: "Whatever the mind of man can conceive and believe, it can achieve." Do you believe it is possible to manifest what you desire? If you do not, create the intention to release any such doubt. It is vital that you have a strong belief that it is possible. When you believe that something is possible, it exists as a probability in the ether. Every thought you think or action you take adds to the weight of that probability until one day, a tipping point is reached. It is like icicles banding together to become a snowflake that falls to earth. It becomes so heavy that it drops down out of the ether into being and voilà! You have manifested your desires. It takes patience, faith, inspiration and action – but it is worth it.

3. Expectancy: Start expecting that the goal will manifest and acting as if it will. This primes the subconscious mind to take appropriate action to ensure that it does. It also magnetises opportunities towards you to help you get what you want.

4. Visualisation: Visualisation stimulates the subconscious mind which is where all change begins. Creatively imagining the goal AS IF IT HAD ALREADY MANIFESTED is the key. It is also vital to tap into the *feeling* of how it is to *have already received* what you want. A powerful guided visualisation is included at the end of this chapter.

5. Action: Because we live in a physical world, you need to take appropriate action to help the goal come into being. So without action, we can "intend" until the cows come home and nothing will change. Whether we want to sell goods or services or change our job, no one else is going to do it for us. No one else CAN do it for us. We may need to advertise or send out a CV or find a business partner. If we want to get published, we need to write to the best of our ability and then find a way to bring our work to the wider world.

    As Maeve Binchy once said in a writing course, if you have written a book, a publisher is not going to come down the chimney and take it out of the drawer and say how wonderful, allow me to publish that! Yes, we are infinite beings – but we live in a physical world. That is why we need to take action – to move our intentions from the mental level to the physical manifestation using the energy of movement to bring our goals out of the ether into the physical world. Some say it needs to be massive action; that sounds scary and overwhelming to me. I don't believe it needs to be massive – it just needs to be appropriate and effective as well as ongoing and consistent. I know from being self-employed that it can be hard to sustain the energy and enthusiasm to constantly offer my work to the public. But what I have found over the years is that when (not if) I get stuck and work dries up, I just need to take action. Any action designed to move things on and get the energy flowing again will do. And then I'm off again until the energy slows again. It goes in a cycle.

6. Surrender: Surrender is not about giving up. It is all about letting go of resistance and worry.

Resistance comes from the ego. The voice of the ego is always negative and discouraging. A better phrase for 'surrender' would be 'delegate.' Once you have done all you can to create your goal, let go and delegate the rest to whatever you conceive of as your Higher Power. Just do your best and let go of the rest.

7. Manifestation: Once we have taken the rest of the steps we need to let go of harassing the Divine to deliver on our schedule. You can't make a healthy plant grow faster than its nature dictates. The things that take time are worth waiting for. Releasing attachment to the when and the how of the outcome shows trust in the Creator. It is a sign of our growth and an implicit acknowledgement that there is something more powerful than us. That there is an invisible presence that is wiser than us, that has our best interests at heart, which can see the big picture. It is useful to assume that the Universe is conspiring to help you. Remember to celebrate your victory which primes the subconscious mind for future success.

In summary, we need to imagine it, give thanks for that which we have already received, have faith, take appropriate action, let go, and then it will manifest.

Gratitude

If we spend what we have on what we need to serve others and serve God, it is replaced instantly.
Rosalyn Bruyere, Healer

Gratitude keeps the heart soft and open, which opens us to allow and receive. Gratitude is high vibration energy and is allied to allowing and attracting. In offering thanks, we redirect our energy from the low vibration of scarcity and raise our ability to attract what we want.

In Conversations with God Book 1, Neale Donald Walsch says (or rather, God says, through him!):

"You will not have that for which you ask, nor can you have anything you want. This is because your very request is a statement of lack, and your saying you want a thing only works to produce that precise experience – wanting – in your reality. The correct prayer is therefore never a prayer of supplication but a prayer of gratitude."[11]

The reason gratitude is a tool of enlightened self-interest is that it is the vibration of ENOUGH. The Universe reflects back to us the exact vibration that we emit. So if we keep asking or wanting, that is what comes back to us, more wanting. We need to let go of imploring God or anyone else for money because asking implies Not Having.

Instead, if we ask the Universe a simple question each day: "What can I do for you today?" then that vibration of generous service comes back to us, with the Universe asking "And how may I serve YOU?" The Universe responds favourably to an exchange of energy because the Principle of Conservation of Energy states, "Energy cannot be created or destroyed, it just changes form."

So when we ask how we can help, and then take action to help, we are offering our energy to the world. It doesn't matter if that is by painting or gardening or working with computers. It's not all about attracting money; no-one ever lay on their death bed and said, "Now that I'm dying, I wish I had more money." What matters is how well we live our lives, and especially, how kind we are to ourselves and all sentient beings, including animals and indeed the earth itself.

The Shape of Help

There is a story of a man stranded on his roof by flood waters. A rescue boat arrives and offers him a lift. "No thanks," he says, "God will rescue me." The waters rise and he gets up on the chimney. A helicopter arrives and offers him a lift. "No thanks," he says, "God will rescue me." He drowns and meets God in heaven. "Why did you not rescue me, God?" he asks. God answers him, exasperated: "What do you think I was trying to do with the boat and the helicopter? Give me a break!"

So something to note is that our help usually comes through other people. Yes, we need to have positive beliefs and intentions to create what we want – but we also need to act on the opportunities that arise for us as a result of those intentions and beliefs. So when the boatman arrives offering help or rescue - say "Yes" and jump in!

Once we get into the flow of giving thanks for what has already arrived, we open ourselves up to synchronicity – the Universe giving us what we seek through apparent coincidence. One time I was getting the kitchen revamped. I got a new radiator put in and because its shape was different from the old one, a section of wallpaper was missing. The wallpaper was nice but had been on the wall for years. I thought, "Where in the world am I going to find a piece to fill that in?" Then I promptly forgot about it and went off for a walk with a dog. In the local park, I brought the dog through a little used area to give her the chance to get lots of new smells. On the ground, wrapped in its original cellophane, was a brand new roll of wallpaper that was exactly what I was looking for. Now that's synchronicity!

Controlling Your Dominant Thought

A mantra or affirmation is a good ally to have when working on creating greater abundance. An affirmation is a positive statement of intent to the self, which needs to be truthful to have power. It is a ready-made positive phrase that reflects what we are working on manifesting. It serves another useful purpose: the mind can only hold one dominant thought at a time. If that dominant thought is positive, there is no room for negative thoughts that can and will attract what we do not want. A useful mantra for manifesting wealth can be:

> *I give thanks that my needs and highest desires are already met with plenty to spare and share.*

What will you allow?

We can only have as much of anything as we will allow, including healing, abundance and love. We don't have to be fearless to live a full life – but we do have to be brave.

I knew a good man who had two young children and was living in a rough housing estate where there were lots of drugs. He was a widower, trying to do his best for his children. He had done a lot of spiritual work on himself and constantly envisioned living in a better house in a better area. He was on the council rehousing list but didn't hold out much hope that he would be rehoused by them, such were the waiting lists. He got a letter one morning, offering him a council house in a much better location. He couldn't believe it and he thought it was a mistake – so he refused it because he didn't want to get into trouble. This is a true story. The only thing scarier than our dreams *not* coming true is our dreams coming true. We may have subconscious abundance blocks or beliefs that sabotage our desire for positive changes.

Visualisation: Attracting and Allowing Abundance

Switch off the phone and make yourself comfortable. Take a deep breath in and as you breathe out, allow your eyes to close. Focus your attention on your breathing. As you breathe in, imagine you are breathing in deep relaxation. As you breathe out, you are beginning to let go. Allow yourself to become quiet inside. Focus your attention behind your eyes and let it rest there......then move your attention up and back and let it rest there....notice how your body relaxes now as your mind slows down.....As you continue to relax, it is easy for you to become aware of the power of your thoughts to create what you want. In this relaxed state of mind, it is easy to let go of old scarcity programming now and make space for new programming of abundance and prosperity.

Imagine you are looking up at a large white cinema screen. On that screen, place a video of you already having become abundant and prosperous. How will you know that you are prosperous? What will you have? What will you be able to do? What positive changes will you make? Make sure the video is in colour, with sound and movement and allow yourself to get excited about the manifestation of your desires. Notice how wonderful it feels! Now from that time in the future where you have already created, allowed and attracted abundance and prosperity, turn and come back to your present moment self, bringing with you a golden piece of advice to help you achieve your heart's desires. That golden piece of advice is now stored in the part of your mind responsible for new learning and new behaviour and it starts affecting your daily life in a positive way from this moment onwards....when you choose to return to the here and now, there is an awareness in your heart that says: I am abundant and prosperous now, with plenty to spare and share.

Chapter 13

Near Death Experiences and Near Life Opportunities

During the NDE, there is an overwhelming understanding that everything is connected.

Dr Penny Sartori

Learning from Death

If loving yourself can teach you anything, it is that we are all worthwhile exactly as we are. The exercise of simple mindfulness can transform your inner landscape so that you experience peacefulness. In that peacefulness the realisation can emerge that we are invisibly interconnected, just like the Internet invisibly connects us all around the globe. Our shared humanity can become real to us. Loving yourself is making contact with your Higher Self. We all have a Higher Self which is an extension of the Divine. Call it Source, God, the field of infinite probabilities – call it whatever you want. It is the same boundless ocean of possibility. By being more loving to ourselves, we go to this ocean with a super tanker to fill instead of a thimble.

Our human lives are finite. What matters is not what we amass but how well we live, and how kind we are to other sentient beings. The field of Near Death Experiences (NDEs) bears this out.

The final clearing out is the letting go of the body. There is no preparation in Western culture for death or dying, which is why so many people are fearful of it. Their fear of death causes them to suffer. Becoming more aware of death is one way to soften the ego. When there is less ego, there is more room for Atman, the pure spiritual self beneath the superficial ego. From my observation as a nurse, a therapist and as a person who has lost loved ones, death is easy. It is the dying part that can be hard.

In her book, Dying to be Me, Anita Moorjani talks of the changes in how she views life since her NDE: *"Previously I used to pursue, feeling as though I had to do, get and achieve.....now, however, I no longer chase anything. Instead, I allow - the more effort I have to put into trying to attain it, the more I know I am doing something wrong. Allowing, on the other hand, doesn't require effort. It feels more like a release, because it means realising that since everything is One, that which I intend to get is already mine."*[12]

In Colm Keane's book, The Distant Shore, there was a consensus from those who had undergone an NDE that *"Love is behind it all. That really is it. We are all part of the spirit of love....It's not just a case of getting by each day and acquiring as much as we can. Physical stuff means nothing. What matters is the way you are with yourself, and with others, your honesty and kindness, and the way you treat other people."*[13]

The overall message from the field of NDE research is that love is the glue that connects us all, it is who we truly are, and at the end of our lives all that matters is how much love we have shared with other sentient beings.

Aligning with our God-Self

> *God's wisdom will fulfil our deepest intentions*
> *once we set them in motion.*
>   Sonia Choquette

Aligning ourselves with spirit requires us to acknowledge that we are part of the Creator Spirit or God, a literal interpretation of being a "child of God." If we accept that we are a child of God, then we are PART of God. We ourselves are part of the divine spark of creation. It is in us, not external to us.

The Higher Self has the overview of our lives. The

soul is consciousness. It knows things that our conscious mind, Lower Self or ego does not know. Like God, it has our best interests at heart. Instead of deconstructing all our fear-based beliefs, a useful shortcut is to hand the running of your life over to your Higher Self. "I now direct my Higher Self to run my life and rule my ego," is a clear command directing this to happen.

This is like handing over all the things we cannot manage, control or fix to a Higher Power. The Higher Power is an extremely competent and trustworthy manager and excellent at handling the details. This then allows you to relax and go with the flow.

A New Way of Being in the World

The journey to loving ourselves is ongoing. Once we love ourselves, we find that we are called to love others more than in the past, and to be of more service. That is because we can only love others to the extent that we love ourselves. This is a natural progression, to steer away from materialism and towards altruism. This improves our life, and the lives of others, whether human or animal.

There are two questions that will keep us on course as we integrate this new way of being in the world.

- How can I be kind to myself and others today?
- What can I do to help others today?

In answering those questions and living the answers, we are creating a better world.

Visualisation: Integrating the Positive Changes

As you continue to relax, allow yourself to enter your safe place, the place of well-being and harmony. Allow yourself to notice what you can see, the vividness of the colours, and the natural beauty all around you. Notice what you can hear…perhaps birdsong, or the sound of silence. Notice how the temperature is perfect for you. And especially, allow yourself to notice how good it feels…in this harmonic place, you have all the time in the world to just relax and be your true self. It feels like a burden has been lifted, to just be you. Or just to…..be…..As you continue to relax even deeper, it is so easy to allow your thoughts to become quiet, easy to ignore. Imagine turning down the volume button on your thoughts now, which in turn lets you realise that you can choose to quieten or ignore those thoughts….this is an idea full of freedom… ..that you can choose which thoughts to focus on, and which ones to act on……………

In this beautiful place, you have a heightened awareness of all the good things and good people already in your life. Your health, your body, your breath, all your blessings… You are aware of the beauty of nature and animals. It is as if you are seeing things in a new, clear way and letting go of the habit of taking things for granted. In this relaxed state, it is so easy to understand that what is truly important is how you treat yourself, nature and all sentient beings with kindness, softness and love….It is as if in releasing and letting go of each breath, you understand at a deep level that softness and surrender are gentle and peaceful and allow space for your deep self to emerge. Your deep and true self is Divine. It is love. In relaxing the body and mind, it is as if you are letting go of struggling upstream against the current, and instead, allowing more flow and ease in your life. Imagine that the safe river is the flow of unconditional love….. imagine now merging with that flow of love in a completely safe and effortless way so that you have a deep inner knowing that you are love, you are loving, you are loved......and it is so easy now to integrate all the positive changes that you have made... this awareness is now stored in the part of your mind responsible for new learning and new behaviour and it starts affecting your daily life in a positive way from this moment onwards. When you choose to return to the here and now, there are two words in your heart: Trust and Hope.

References

1. O'Doherty, Michael, Bio-Energy Healing, O'Brien Press, 1991
2. Pert, Candace, Molecules of Emotion, Scribner, 1997
3. Lipton, Bruce, The Biology of Belief, Hay House 2005
4. Lobel, Thalma, Sensation: The New Science of Physical Intelligence, Icon, 2014
5. Chodron, Pema, The Places that Scare Us, Element, 2003
6. Yeats, William Butler, 'The Lake Isle of Inishfree,' The Poems, Everyman, 1994
7. Choquette, Sonia, Walking Home, Hay House, 2014
8. McTaggart, Lynne, The Field, Element, 2003
9. Pascal, Blaise, Pascal in a Nutshell, Hodder & Stoughton, 1997
10. Moorjani, Anita, Dying to be Me, Hay House, 2012
11. Walsch, Neale Donald, The Complete Conversations with God, G.P. Putnam's Sons, 2005
12. Moorjani, Anita, Dying to be Me, Hay House, 2012
13. Keane, Colm, The Distant Shore, Capel Island, 2010

Suggested Reading and Resources

The meditations in this book have been professionally recorded and are available to purchase for download. For more information visit www.maresehickey.com

Feel free to visit Marese's blog and website on www.maresehickey.com and receive the gift of a meditation download called "Letting Go and Feeling Good" when you sign up for emails about new releases.

The Teachings of Silver Birch, Editor A.W. Austen, Spiritual Truth Press 2014.

The Honeymoon Effect, Bruce Lipton, Hay House 2013.

Energy Psychology www.eftfree.net

The Wisdom of NDEs, Dr Penny Sartori, Watkins 2014

The Divine Matrix, Gregg Braden, Hay House 2007

Acknowledgements

This book would not have made it out of the starting gate without a lot of help. Thank you to my writing buddy Dolores O'Malley, for all the tea and the writing work we did together. Thank you to the following people for their encouragement, and their time spent reading it and suggesting changes: Veron Bennett, Emma Champ, Maeve and Jerry O'Dwyer, Kate O'Malley, Sheila Whyte, and Olive O'Sullivan.

CPSIA information can be obtained
at www.ICGtesting.com
Printed in the USA
LVOW12s1622180416
484151LV00001B/24/P

9 781523 264650